BOAT DIVER
MANUAL

Acknowledgments

Editor in Chief
Drew Richardson, Ed.D.

Instructional Design, Development, Consultation and Review
Lesley Alexander, Ph.D.; Lori Bachelor-Smith; Mark Caney; Pascal Dietrich; Heather Goodwin-Robinson; Mike Holme; Yasushi Inoue; John Kinsella; Ted Moreta; Steve Mortell; Suzanne Pleydell; Julie Taylor Sanders; Karl Shreeves, M.A.; Trond Skaare; Linda Van Velsan; LeRoy Wickham

Graphic Design and Production
Janet Klendworth, Caroline Vu

Illustrations
Janet Klendworth

Photography
Karl Shreeves

Production and Coordination
Lori Bachlor-Smith, Heather Goodwin-Robinson, Ted Moreta, Dawn Azua, Joshua Stewart

A special thanks to Florida Keys Dive Center, Ocean Divers and the *Sundiver* for their support and services. Thanks to the Aggressor Fleet for stock photography.

Boat Diver *Manual*

Published by PADI
30151 Tomas Street
Rancho Santa Margarita, CA 92688-2125

ISBN 978-1-878663-80-1

Printed in USA

Product No. 79170 (09/10) Version 1.02 102PDH10

Table of Contents

SCUBAPRO
Achilles
CF 0851 J

Introduction

It's a beautiful day. The sun's high, glinting off the water as you and several of your dive buddies head out to sea. You may be on a charter dive boat – one of several buddy teams and groups – or it may just be you and your friends smashing through waves with an outboard inflatable. Either way, it's going to be a great day of underwater adventure and boating fun.

If you're a diver, chances are you've already been boat diving. If you haven't, it's almost inevitable because you reach some of the best diving by boat. At some dive destinations, all the diving is boat diving. Considering this, it's hard to separate boating and diving in most contexts. Becoming a PADI Boat Diver is a natural step in being a diver.

The PADI Boat Diver Specialty course teaches the basic principles for fun, safe diving from boats, and provides you an overview of boating procedures and practices. The course was designed for flexibility, so that what you learn applies to diving from large charter dive boats in tropical water or small private vessels in temperate climates. This course should help you get more out of boat diving, whether you're motivated to do so as a means to an end (to get to the dive site) or for the fun boating offers in itself.

Course Overview

As with most PADI Specialty Diver courses, the PADI Boat Diver course emphasizes diving, and you will make a least two boat dives in open water with your PADI Instructor. You'll have fun on these dives while developing and refining the skills you need for boat diving.

Although the PADI Boat Diver course isn't a boating course, it includes significant background information that helps you understand not just diving from a boat, but what it takes to safely operate a boat. Normally you'll cover this information by reading this manual, by watching the PADI *Boat Diving* video, and by discussing the material with your instructor prior to your dives. Your instructor may decide to have more formal class meetings and/or practice sessions. The recommended sequence is to begin by skimming through this manual, noting the headings, topics and pictures. This speeds learning by giving you an idea of where you're headed. Then, as you read, highlight or underline the answers to the study objectives. **It's important to actually do this** - not simply note them - because the physical act of writing/highlighting enhances transferring the knowledge to long term memory. Answer the exercises, reviewing anything you don't understand. Then, fill out the Knowledge Reviews to turn in to your instructor.

After completing the manual, watch the *Boat Diving* video. This reinforces what you read, and shows demonstrations of many of the skills you'll learn. You'll also get to see many aspects of vessel operation from a captain's point of view. If you prefer to watch the video first, that's fine.

You may initially practice some of the skills you'll learn in controlled conditions, such as gearing up and entering the water from a boat. Your instructor may add a pool or confined water dive for added time to develop skills before your boat dives.

When you've completed the course, you'll have earned the PADI Boat Diver certification, which qualifies you to boat dive in conditions comparable to or better than those in which you have experience and training. With your PADI Boat Diver certification, you can apply for the Master Scuba Diver rating if you also have the PADI Rescue Diver certification, and four other PADI specialty certifications.

The PADI Boat Diver certification credits toward the PADI Master Scuba Diver rating - recreational diving's highest nonprofessional level.

Other Skills You'll Want as a PADI Boat Diver

Boat diving skills integrate well with the skills you develop to enjoy new opportunities through training in other PADI Specialty Diver courses.

- PADI Enriched Air Diver - Enriched air nitrox extends your no stop times, which can be particularly handy in boat diving situations that have relatively short surface intervals. By using EANx, you have a longer repetitive dive for a given surface interval.
- PADI Deep Diver - One advantage of diving from boats is that they take you places that can be hard or impossible to reach by shore diving. In some areas, this includes deeper dive sites. PADI Deep Diver training prepares you to fully enjoy diving at these sites.
- PADI Diver Propulsion Vehicle (DPV) Diver - DPVs are a lot of fun to drive and expand the area you can see on a dive. Boats are the ideal platform for DPV diving because, even with the larger models, it's relatively easy to enter and exit the water with them. Although you can DPV dive from shore in many places, the combination of DPV and boat is a natural.
- PADI Peak Performance Buoyancy Diver - It's useful to fine tune your buoyancy skills. When you're neutrally buoyant you use less air so you can safely extend your bottom time. In addition, good buoyancy control minimizes incidental contact with your surrounding helping you protect the sensitive marine organisms or fragile parts of shipwrecks.
- The first dive of most PADI specialties* corresponds to the same dive in the PADI Adventures in Diving program. Therefore, if you're a PADI Advanced Open Water Diver or Adventure Diver, you may have already made the first dive to these specialty courses. Similarly, the first dive of the specialties credits toward the Advanced Open Water Diver or Adventure Diver certification.
- Successfully completing five PADI Specialties and the PADI Rescue Diver course qualifies you for the PADI Master Scuba Diver rating - the highest nonprofessional rating in the sport.

For more information about PADI courses, including specialties, the Adventures in Diving program and PADI Master Scuba Diver, visit padi.com.

**A few specialties such as PADI Ice Diver and PADI Cavern Diver do not have corresponding specialty dives.*

Watch for These Symbols

Alerts you to important safety information. Pay close attention when you see this symbol and consult your instructor if you do not understand the material.

Reminds you to interact harmoniously with the aquatic environment while highlighting relevant information or a specific diving technique.

Alerts you to additional/related information on PADI videos, books, CD-ROM and other media. This material is for your interest and further learning. The information required for this course is in this manual.

The Advantages of *Boat Diving*

Study Objectives

Underline/highlight the answer to this question as you read:

1. What are five advantages of diving from a boat?

If you've been boat diving before, you undoubtedly already recognize several advantages. Most divers enjoy diving from boats for one or all of the following five reasons:

1. Diving from a boat gives you opportunities to dive in areas you could not otherwise reach. Many excellent dive sites lie well beyond a reasonable swim from shore access – sometimes many kilometres/miles from it. Without a boat, you'll never get to these sites. In other areas, dive sites are within reach of shore, but you don't have access to that shore, either due to logistics (an excessive walk, dense growth, etc.) or legal access (private property, restricted area, etc.). In these cases as well, it's either dive from a boat or never see them.

2. Boat diving allows you to seek out the calmest and clearest waters. You can do this shore diving, too, but when conditions are poor at your primary dive site, it's often much easier to find decent conditions via boat. When you're shore diving in most places, the same stretch of coast will have similar conditions. With a boat, however, you can check out an offshore reef if you're inshore or vice versa. You may be able to cruise to the lee side of an island or other obstacle that provides cover from a rough sea. In addition, when looking for better conditions, you can easily evaluate as you go, whereas this isn't so easy by automobile.

3. Boat diving is typically easier than shore diving. While there are certainly many very convenient shore dives, it's hard to beat boat diving for convenience. The longest walk you have in your gear on a boat dive is never more than a few steps, and your entry typically consists of a single giant stride or a back roll. After the dive, you usually climb a short ladder or slip out of your gear and hop up on the boat's side. Because the boat's usually over the dive site, or at least very close, long surface swims are seldom necessary.

4. Less wear and tear on your equipment. Compared to most (but certainly not all) shore diving, boat diving causes less wear, especially regarding your wet suit boots and exposure suit knees. This is because you're walking or on your knees much less when boat diving than when diving from shore.

5. Boat diving is fun because there's social interaction. Probably the best reason to boat dive is that it's fun. It's a great way to spend time with your friends in a setting that's both adventurous and relaxing at the same time. Diving from charter dive boats is also an excellent way to meet new dive buddies and make new friends.

It's hard to beat boat diving for convenience, and generally speaking, boat diving causes less wear and tear on your gear.

Exercise 1 - The Advantages of Boat Diving

1. Reasons for boat diving compared to shore diving include (check all that apply):
   - ☐ a. opportunities to visit places you can't reach from shore.
   - ☐ b. the ability to seek the calmest and clearest water.
   - ☐ c. it is typically easier than shore diving.
   - ☐ d. it's fun because you spend time with friends and make new ones.

How'd you do?
1. a, b, c, d.

Boat *Terminology*

Study Objectives

Underline/highlight the answers to these questions as you read:

1. What are a boat's *bow* (*forward*), *stern* (*astern, aft*), *starboard* side and *port* side?
2. Which is the *windward* side and which is the *leeward* side of a boat?
3. What do the following terms refer to on a boat: *head, galley, bridge, wheelhouse* (or *pilothouse*), *transom, rail, cylinder racks, bunks* (*staterooms*), and *diving entry/exit area*?

Even if you've never been aboard a boat or ship, from movies, television, novels or the internet, you're probably aware that the captain and crew frequently use nautical terms for different directions and parts of the boat. Some terms are important because they avoid any confusion (especially with respect to direction,) whereas other terms hang on primarily from tradition, and yet others fall somewhere in between. Either way, realize that boat terminology is not arbitrary, and if a particular term is still around due to tradition, at least it originated for a practical reason. Since you'll be aboard boats, understanding the terminology helps you understand what someone's saying – which is especially important if the person's talking to *you*.

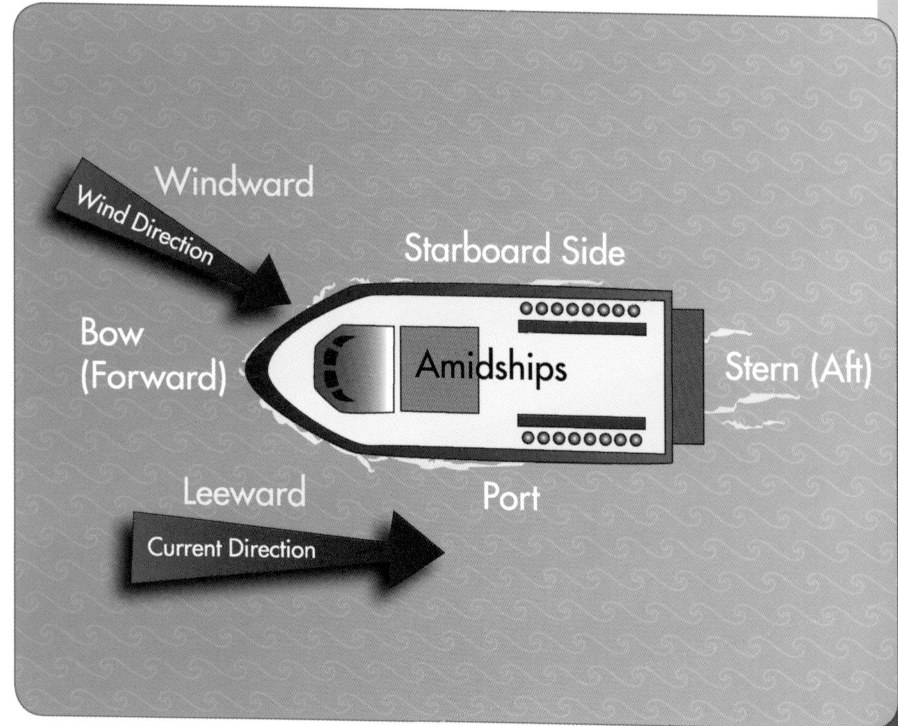

Common boat terms

Orientation Terms

Common directional terms like right and left can be confusing on a boat. If someone is facing the captain and yells "Watch out for the reef on the right!" does that mean the captain's right or the yelling person's right? To avoid this, on board a boat you use terms relative to the boat, facing the bow.

The *bow* is the front end, or *forward* part of the boat. When someone says "meet on the bow," it means up close to the vessel's pointed end. If someone says "go forward," that means toward the bow, though it's a looser reference. The prefix *fore* means forward, such as foredeck, which means the deck near the front of the boat.

The *stern* is the back end of the boat, with *astern* or *aft* meaning toward the back of the boat. A crewmember yelling "all clear astern" is telling the captain everything's clear behind the boat. A reference to the aft deck is a reference to the deck near the stern.

Starboard means the right side of the boat, and *port* means the left side of the boat. Incidentally, *starboard* comes from *steer-board*, a reference to early vessels that had their rudder (steering board) on the right side because most people are right handed. It helps to remember these terms by remembering that *port* and *left* both have four letters.

You may combine orientation terms to give a more precise reference. For instance, to say you see divers on *port bow* means that you see them on the left side of the front of the boat.

Amidships means the middle of the vessel, and can refer to the center relative to fore and aft, or relative to port and starboard, depending upon context. A pilot saying "rudder amidships" is saying the ship's rudder is straight – aligned parallel between port and starboard. A crewmember yelling that a hat blew overboard "starboard amidships" is saying that the hat is off the boat's right side, about the center.

Aloft means overhead, in a mast or in the rigging of a sailboat, whereas below means *below* the deck. If say you're "going below," you mean you're going down inside the decks. *Above deck* means being on the deck, or *ondeck*.

Windward and *leeward* (often pronounced "loo-ard") are directions relative to the wind rather than to the boat. Windward is the side or direction toward, or up wind, and leeward is the side or direction away from or downwind. These were understandably important concepts in the days of sail, but remain so in the age of powered boats because the wind affects maneuvering and how a boat sits while moored, among other things.

Areas and Things

Besides direction, you identify specific locations on a boat and parts of the vessel with nautical terminology. We'll cover the most common of these, but there are others, so if you hear a term you don't understand, be sure to ask what it means.

The *head* means both the boat's toilet – the actual apparatus – and the restroom facility in general. On most dive boats, the head is not much like the toilet in your house, and is actually a highly specialized pump. Accordingly, it's important not to put anything in the head except material that's passed through your body and a small amount of toilet tissue (and sometimes even the tissue's not allowed in there). To prevent some unpleasant inconveniences and falling into disfavor with the crew or boat owner, always follow directions regarding the head.

The *galley* is a boat's kitchen, and the *bridge* is a raised platform from which the helmsman (pilot) steers the boat. The elevation allows the pilot to see a larger area from the elevated vantage point. The *wheelhouse* or *pilot house* is an enclosure for the boat pilot, usually with the ships *wheel* (steering wheel), compass and other instruments. The **wheelhouse** and the bridge may be the same thing, and many vessels have two sets of controls

– an elevated bridge and a more protected wheelhouse or wheelhouse-like area.

The *transom* is the planking that forms the stern of a square ended boat. On small boats, such as inflatables, the outboard motor attaches to the transom. The *rail* is a guard or barrier at the outer edge of the deck. The rail, if the boat has one, is mounted on the *gunwale* (pronounced "gunnel"), which is the upper edge of the side of the boat. On an inflatable boat, for example, the top of the pontoon is considered the gunwale.

Cylinder racks are any of various stands used for storing and securing scuba cylinders. On most dive boats, they're designed so that you can set up your scuba unit and keep the cylinder in the rack. Some cylinder racks require you to secure the cylinders with a loop of bungee or by some other means. Cylinders should always be secured when aboard, except when you're using them, have contact and can make sure they don't fall, tumble or roll.

On most dive boats, cylinder racks are designed so that you can set up your scuba unit and keep the cylinder in the rack. Cylinders should always be secured when aboard, except when you're using them, have contact and can make sure they don't fall, tumble or roll.

You won't find *bunks* (beds) or *staterooms* (sleeping quarters) on many dive boats, but in some areas they're common. They range from bunks with curtains to small cabins that afford a bit more space and privacy.

The diving entry/exit areas are those areas designated for you to enter and exit the water. On many boats, you enter and exit the same place – typically the stern – but with others, you enter and exit different areas. Large dive boats on the west coast of the United States, for example, commonly have divers enter from the sides and exit up the stern.

Nautical Name Fun

Here are some nautical terms you may not have heard, and some you have but may not know where they came from. Many are tongue-in-cheek, and unofficial, yet you'll hear them used.

Bear Up – To steer a sailboat so that the bow stays away from the wind so the sails stay full and the boat continues to make way. It has fallen into common use meaning "keep up your morale."

Belay – To secure or tie something so it can't move. It also means to stop or secure what you're doing.

Blazer – A brightly colored jacket. The name comes from the *HMS Blazer*, 1845, the crew of which dressed in bright blue and white jackets.

Calling Up Ralph – To get seasick.

Cast Iron Wind – A sailboat's motor.

Gunwale – The uppermost side of a boat, so named because old ships had their guns mounted there.

Perks – Royal Navy abbreviation for "perquisites," meaning special privileges or accommodations for particular offices. This is where we get the term "perks" meaning "benefits."

Posh – Upper class and better. The term is said to have originated as the acronym POSH, which stood for Port Outward, Starboard Home. The P & O Steam Navigation Company allocated the upper class cabins accordingly in the Red Sea because they were cooler, with POSH stamped on the tickets.

Rabbits – Private items you plan to take ashore. The term originally referred to small items smuggled ashore by sailors or ship passengers.

Exercise 2 - Boat Terminology

1. If the captain says there's an object floating off the port bow, you would look off the ____________ side of the boat:

   ☐ a. front, right.

   ☐ b. front, left.

   ☐ c. rear, right.

   ☐ d. rear, left.

2. If you're on the side of the boat that the wind's coming from, you're on the __________ side.

   ☐ a. starboard

   ☐ b. leeward

   ☐ c. port

   ☐ d. windward

3. The head is a boat's ____ and the wheelhouse is the _________.

   ☐ a. restroom, kitchen

   ☐ b. kitchen, steering area

   ☐ c. stern planking, restroom

   ☐ d. restroom, steering area

How'd you do?
1. b. 2. d. 3. d

Types of *Boats*

Study Objectives

Underline/highlight the answers to these questions as you read:

1. What three features do you expect from virtually any dive boat?
2. What are the four general dive boat categories and their characteristics?
3. What are the local boating laws and regulations specific to: a) boat ownership, b) registration, c) numbering and d) documentation?

If it floats and carries a person, it's probably been at least tried as a dive platform. Today, boat diving takes place from vessels ranging from small ships to single person sit-on-top ocean kayaks. Small runabouts, motorsailers, sailboats, pontoon boats, and luxury yachts have all been used to support diving. Diving from the largest live-aboard dive boats may involve diving from the live-aboard itself and from its smaller support boats, depending upon the dive site and where the vessel moors.

Dive Boat Features

Whether a racing yacht or run-of-the-mill rowboat, there are three features that you expect from a good dive vessel: ample deck space, stability and power. What you mean by each of these depends partly on the situation, so that a boat can be an excellent dive vessel in one environment, and a very poor one in another.

Ample deck space. Diving takes up a lot of room, so you want ample space for your gear, setting it up and getting into it. Sometimes, a smaller vessel with more deck space is a far better choice for diving than an equal or larger boat that lacks deck space due to features or luxuries. A good example would be two medium-small inflatable boats (about 5 metres/15 feet long), one with a center wheel console and one with a basic tiller outboard. The one with the basic outboard may not be as comfortable to operate, but will have much more deck space.

What you mean by "ample" also depends upon how diving takes place. In some areas, you set up all your gear, load it aboard and put on your exposure suit before you leave the dock for a short ride to the dive site. After the dive, your gear stays together and you stay suited up until you return. In this case, you don't need as much space as if you're going to be out on the boat all day and must set everything up and gear up on the water.

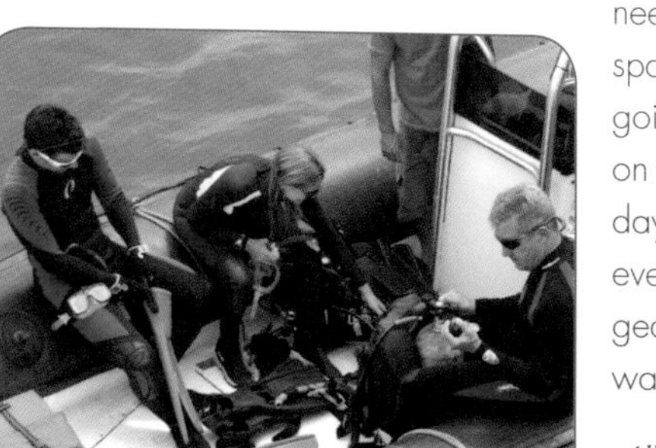

All things being equal, a boat with more deck space makes a better platform for diving.

Stability. Dive boats must be as stable as reasonably possible so you can maintain your balance standing (on larger boats) with gear on, to minimize the potential for equipment to roll about, and for passenger comfort. Again, stability is a relative term. Even in rough conditions, even a relatively stable boat isn't that stable. Likewise, a boat with only marginal stability characteristics may be more than adequate for the smooth water you find on lakes or in protected bays and waterways.

In designing a boat, there's a trade between stability and seaworthiness. A vessel that rolls easily is said to be tender, and all else being equal, a tender vessel is less likely to capsize in large waves than is a more stable vessel. However, a vessel can be very tender due to poor design or improper loading, in which case it can be both tender and unstable. Fortunately, design issues aren't common in modern vessels and loads shouldn't be issues when the crew observes load requirements (found on the boat capacity plate, usually placed near the wheel).

From a practical sense, most charter dive boats and most popular private boats are relatively stable and have excellent seaworthiness. When conditions are beyond what these vessels can safely handle, you're not likely to be out diving anyway.

Power. Dive gear adds a good bit of weight compared to hauling the same number of passengers without it, so a dive boat needs to have ample power to move the weight in the most demanding conditions (waves, current, wind) you're reasonably likely to face. The boat also needs adequate power to reach and maintain a reasonable speed should it be necessary to transport an injured diver.

Again, this is relative. If you're going a short distance over smooth water, a very small engine may be more than adequate. In some places, it's common for seven or eight people to dive from 4 metre/12 foot boats propelled by 10 to 15 horsepower engines. On the other hand, for example, the large inflatable dive boats used in the North Atlantic and Mediterranean have comparatively more power for their weight so they move reliably and quickly through rough seas and against wind and current while fully loaded. These vessels commonly have twin engines with more than 100 horsepower combined.

Dive gear adds a good bit of weight, requiring an engine with ample power to move it.

Dive Boat Categories

Because there are many different types of vessels suited to many different aquatic environments, you could create perhaps dozens of descriptions to categorize them. For the purposes of this course, though, we can generalize more and use four basic categories based on broad characteristics they share.

Inflatables. In many areas, inflatables are popular as private and charter dive boats. They're also commonly used as support and safety boats for larger vessels. Inflatables suited to diving range from 3 metres/10 feet to more than 5 metres/15 feet long. Their design consists (basically) of two air-filled tubes that meet at the bow, and connected at the rear by a solid transom for an outboard (or two). In most modern inflatables, the inflated tubes sub divide into smaller compartments so that the boat remains afloat even with a major puncture. Diving inflatables have a solid floor suited to diving.

There are two basic inflatable designs – the fabric hull/inflatable keel design and the rigid hull/solid keel. The fabric hull/inflatable keel design came first because the original idea was to have a boat that you could deflate, fold up and store or transport without a trailer, yet that could handle a relatively powerful engine and take on rough seas. Inflatables quickly proved to be very stable and seaworthy, which led to the rigid hull/solid keel inflatable boats (often called RIBs – Rigid Inflatable Boats). These inflatables can't be folded up and require trailers out of water, but use the inflatable design for the tremendous stability and seaworthiness it provides. The solid hull and keel gives it superior handling performance, especially in rough water. Both designs are rugged and among the most seaworthy vessels for their size.

Smaller inflatables used for diving usually have a simple tiller outboard (pilot sits at the rear and steers with a handle mounted directly on the outboard). This no-frills approach leaves the deck open for maximum space. Larger inflatables, which have more deck space to work with, more commonly have central control stations to provide a more comfortable piloting station.

Smaller inflatables used for diving usually have a tiller outboard to keep the deck space open.

Larger inflatables usually have a center control console and still provide ample deck space for divers.

Hard-hull day boats. This is a very large category that includes resort pontoon flattops, runabouts, utility boats, small sailboats and skiffs. For dive purposes, they range from about 5 metres/15 feet to more than 6 metres/20 feet, and may have outboard engines (mounted on the transom) or inboard/inboard-outboard engines (mounted inside the hull with the propeller shaft routed out of the hull through a watertight fitting).

The best boats for diving in this category are those with ample deck space. There are models designed specifically for fishing and diving with this in mind. Boats intended for touring or racing, on the other hand, often have relatively limited deck space and may be inconvenient with respect to diving.

Live-aboards are boats upon which you eat, sleep and dive from for two or more days. This category includes vessels that could *be used for this, even if they're not.*

Cabin cruisers. This category includes cabin cruisers, medium sized sailboats, yachts and many small dive charter boats that hold six to ten divers. The distinction between smaller cabin cruisers and the larger hard-hull day boats is admittedly a gray area, but for our purposes, cabin cruisers are vessels ranging from approximately 6 metres/20 feet to around 9 metres/28 feet (which is the approximately largest size that may be trailered conventionally in the U.S. and many other countries). Smaller vessels in this category may have outboard engines, but most have inboard/inboard-outboard engines. The term *cruiser* suggests that this type of boat has at least minimum accommodations and facilities for an overnight trip.

As you'd expect, the best cabin cruisers for diving are those with lots of deck space. Power isn't usually an issue with these vessels, because by design most have ample power.

The best cabin cruisers for diving are those with lots of deck spa.

Live-aboards. In diving, the term live-aboard commonly refers to vessels upon which you eat, sleep and from which you dive over a period of two or more days. For the purposes of this discussion, this category includes all vessels that *could* be used for this purpose, even though many are not.

Live-aboards range from approximately 9 metres/30 feet to more than 100 metres/330 feet and include converted commercial fishing vessels, large charter dive boats, luxurious yachts and even cruise ships. Some of the largest are so big divers shuttle to and from the dive site in inflatables or smaller, hard-hull day boats rather than diving from the vessel itself.

Boats in this category make up the majority of the large charter dive boats common to the most popular dive areas. They can carry more than 10 divers, up to 50 or even more when catering to snorkelers. When used for day charters, the accommodations are usually more minimal and it's possible to carry more divers. Those used for overnight stays dedicate more below deck space to bunks, heads, etc., but typically can't have as many divers for overnight trips.

Boats in the live-aboard category make up the majority of large charter dive boats common to the most popular dive areas.

Local Laws and Regulations

Governments regulate boats and boating in virtually all parts of the world today, especially when paying passengers and carrying cargo are involved. Laws and regulations relating to boats vary widely, and your instructor will brief you on those that apply in your area.

Generally speaking, in most countries and territories, boats have titles of ownership, much like automobiles. This provides a legal record of not only who owns the boat, in most jurisdictions, who has a lien on it, such as a lender in the case of a loan financing the boat. Boats are usually registered, with numbers for the registration typically placed on both sides of the bow. This is similar to the registration and corresponding license plate found on automobiles. Documentation of the registration is usually required to be aboard and available to law enforcement officials.

Besides these requirements, commercial vessels (such as dive charter boats) typically need a commercial license, and the captain has to qualify and have a license to carry paying passengers. Both boat and captain's licenses may have limits, such as the number of passengers the boat may carry, or the maximum vessel size the captain may operate. You can find more

Decline of Two-Stroke Engine

For many years, two-stroke gasoline (petrol) outboard engines were very popular, and for good reasons. Compared to more common four-stroke engines (as typically found in your automobile) they generate more horsepower for an engine of a given weight. Because two-stroke engines have oil added to the fuel (manually or automatically), oil coats the internal workings and the exhaust, providing (as a by-product) a measure of corrosion protection in the salt water environment.

More recently, however, the two stroke has fallen into disfavor and they are even banned in some areas. The reason is that compared to four stroke motors, two strokes produce more waste, dumping (by some estimates) as much as 25 to 30 percent of the fuel consumed into the exhaust. This fuel and the oil added to it get into the water when used in aquatic applications. With the rise of four stroke outboard (and other small application) engines with good horsepower, two strokes are being phased out wherever possible in favor of a cleaner environment.

information about these legal requirements by visiting the websites of or contacting the office of the local government bodies that regulate boats.

Popular Websites for Boating Laws & Regulations

Australian Maritime Safety Authority www.amsa.gov.au

Canadian Office of Boating Safety www.tc.gc.ca/BoatingSafety

European Boating Association www.eba.com

Maritime New Zealand www.govt.nz

Tokyo Sail and Power Squadron www.tspsjapan.org

UK Royal Yachting Association www.rya.org.uk

UK Maritime & Coastguard Agency www.mcga.gov.uk

US Coast Guard Office of Boating Safety www.uscgboating.org

US Power Squadron www.usps.org

Exercise 3 - Types of Boats

1. The features you expect from virtually any dive boat include (check all that apply):
   - ☐ a. center console.
   - ☐ b. ample deck space.
   - ☐ c. power.
   - ☐ d. stability.

2. The _______ category of dive boat is characterized as ____________.
   - ☐ a. yacht, lacking deck space
   - ☐ b. inflatable, consisting of two inflated tubes that join at the bow
   - ☐ c. power boat, having a small inboard engine
   - ☐ d. cruise ship, needing a large anchor

3. Laws and regulations specific to boat ownership, registration, numbering and documentation are only found in a few limited places worldwide.

   ☐ True ☐ False

How'd you do?

1. b, c, d. a is not correct because smaller dive boats often lack the console to maximize deck space. 2. b. 3. False. Almost all countries and territories have laws and regulations specific to boat ownership, registration, numbering and documentation.

Boating Basics *for Divers*

Study Objectives

Underline/highlight the answers to these questions as you read:

1. What are the basic international rules of the road?
2. What are the common, local navigational aids?
3. What are navigational charts and why are they important?
4. What navigational instruments do you use to navigate a boat?
5. What considerations apply to when a dive boat leaves and returns to the dock?

The Rules of the Road

Even in flat calm conditions, operating a boat differs from driving a car in that the "road" extends in all directions and in most places, there are no lanes constraining where a vessel can go. Therefore, boats can approach you from any direction, and you can find yourself approaching one boat while another is crossing at your bow and another is crossing obliquely astern. To avoid collisions and to allow everyone to progress smoothly and safely, boat operators follow the "rules of the road" that govern who makes way and who must yield when boats meet in open water. Just as streets have signs and warnings you obey as a motorist, inshore waterways often have beacons and markings that control traffic and direct you away from hazards.

Although different areas have differing nuances with respect to rules of the road, the principles you'll learn as a PADI Boat Diver are the basic ones that apply internationally. Your instructor will brief you on local variations. For example, navigation rules encompass lighting requirements for every description of watercraft. In most countries, power driven and sailing vessels less than 20 metres/66 feet are equipped with green lights on their starboard side and red lights on their port side. It's important to note however, that the green/red lights on the starboard/port sides may be the other way around in some countries.

Keep in mind that this is a boat *diving* course, not a boating course, and this discussion isn't intended to qualify you to operate a boat. Rather, you learn these basics so you can understand and recognize how and why the captain and crew operate their vessel the way they do, and how it relates to your safety. Diving from boats is more interesting if you have a basic background in boating. It can also be quite practical information to know in the event you need to assist on board in an emergency, or if you plan to operate your own craft. If you're interested in qualifying as a private or commercial boat captain, complete a locally sanctioned course in boat operations.

Vessel to starboard makes way. The first principle you learn in boating is that when two vessels approach each other so their paths will cross, the vessel to the starboard makes *way*, i.e., making way and is called the *stand on* vessel. The vessel to port is *burdened* and must maneuver or slow to allow the other vessel to continue on course. The vessel with way should maintain its course and speed so the burdened vessel can avoid it more easily.

When two boats approach each other, the one to starboard makes way. The vessel to port must slow or alter course to allow the starboard vessel to continue its course.

You can think of the area from bow amidships down the entire starboard side as the "danger zone" in which any approaching vessel makes way. The captain or pilot watches around the entire vessel, but watches this area especially because boats in this zone are the ones that legally require maneuvering to avoid.

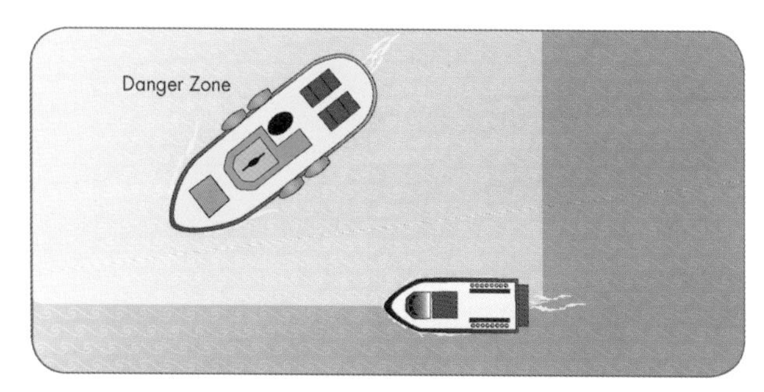

Any vessel in the "danger zone" makes way.

If you watch closely, you'll often notice that the captain does not maneuver or change speed as another boat crosses the bow from the starboard side, and that vessel passes with ample safe space. How does the captain know that they weren't on a close course or a collision course?

You can determine a collision course by watching the relative position of an approaching vessel – if it doesn't change, you're on a collision course. So if you see, for example, a boat approaching and it remains exactly off the same point on the starboard bow, and it's still there as you get closer, your vessel needs to alter speed or direction. If, on the other hand, its relative position shifts so that it's closer to the bow or farther from the bow, then you know it will pass ahead or astern, respectively. If the relative position is changing but very slowly (and the vessel is close), then there's still some risk of a collision or passing too close for safety, and your vessel must give way. By the way, this relative position principle works with any two moving vehicles, including airplanes and motor vehicles.

Exceptions to the rule. To keep things interesting, there are some exceptions to which vessel is burdened. A sailboat under sail makes way over a boat under power, even if the sailboat approaches from port. A sailboat under power is treated the same as any power boat, and when two sailboats under sail approach each other, the one to starboard makes way.

Another exception is "might makes right," which is to say that relatively small, maneuverable vessels accommodate very large, cumbersome vessels regardless of the usual rules. Even a large charter boat is considered small and maneuverable compared to an oil tanker, and would almost always accommodate the tanker if they approached each other near a harbor entrance, for example. While this is an informal rule in most areas, it's widely recognized and applied because the smaller vessel can stay clear of the larger one much more easily than vice versa, and because the reality is a large freighter could crush and sink a hard-hull day boat without the freighter's captain or crew knowing it happened.

Finally, vessels that *cannot* maneuver makes way, irrespective of size. Commercial fishing boats putting down or taking up nets are one example. A dive boat flying the Alpha (blue and white) dive flag while accompanying drift divers also makes way, legally speaking.

Head on approaches. There are rules for when vessels approach head on so that two vessels don't hit because they're trying to evade each other. As a matter of historical interest, it was confusion over following these rules that led to the *Stockholm* striking the *Andrea Doria* in 1956 (there's still dispute over who was at fault), despite the fact that both vessels were alone in a huge ocean and trying to miss each other. The rule, generally, is that vessels pass port to port, or "keep right and you'll be right." This is a general rule, however, in that two vessels may pass starboard to starboard when, for example, they're adequately separated and it's obvious that's what they're going to do to both captains.

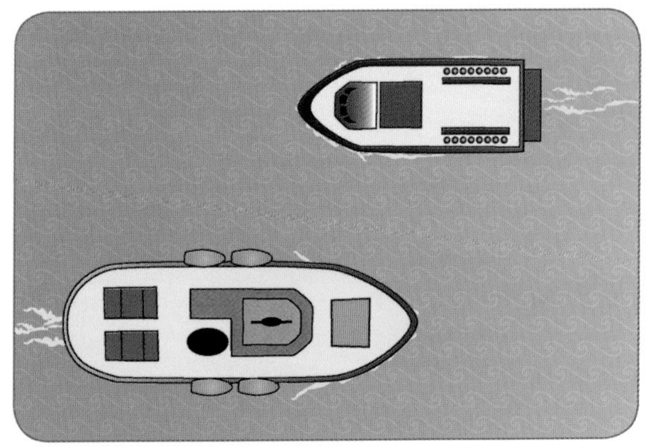

The general rule is that vessels pass each other port side to port side.

Despite these rules, circumstances and conditions sometimes make it hard for the captains of their respective vessels to understand what the other intends to do. When this happens, captains communicate. They can do this by radio, gestures or a horn blast, but more often it's making a clear, early deliberate maneuver in a safe direction that reveals a clear intention to the other captain. In these situations, it's important to avoid subtle, hard to detect course changes because the other vessel may not recognize and adjust accordingly.

Overtaking. When two vessels are headed the same way and the one astern wishes to pass the one ahead, it signals with its horn (two long and one short blast) and passes along the starboard after the forward vessel replies with a single blast. Inland rules differ slightly here with giving one short blast of the horn if passing to starboard, or two short blasts if passing to port and the vessel to be passed replies in same to acknowledge a starboard or a port passing.

Duty to avoid collisions. The last rule of the road is a "catch all" that keeps everyone responsible and reasonable. All vessels have a duty to avoid collisions, regardless of circumstances, including giving way if necessary when the other vessel is supposed to be burdened. This is especially true where there are many recreational boaters, many of whom due to inexperience are more likely to confuse or fail to recognize who makes way. Therefore, after a collision, having way, by itself, is not an adequate defense.

Common Navigational Aids

Just as you have signs on the road that direct you when you operate a motor vehicle, there are common navigational aids that direct your path and help you avoid hazards when boating. These take several forms, depending upon the use and where they're placed

Buoys. (sea marks) are any of many floating devices used to aid piloting by marking a channel, hazard or administrative area (such as mooring zone, swimming area, etc.). Buoys are typically color-coded and often shape coded to tell you what they mean, and many have their meaning stenciled onto them as well. Among other uses, buoys are used as channel markers (along with pilings jutting up from the sea floor), with red and green used to mark the channel. In most countries the usual convention is to have green on the starboard side when outbound and red on the starboard side when inbound (think "red-right-return"). In some countries however, it's exactly the other way around. Returning from sea, the green markers are on your right, or starboard, and the red are on your left, your port side, and between is the channel. In most areas, the green markers, are cylindrical buoys or rectangular signs (on pilings), and the red are on pointed buoys or triangular signs. These are sometimes called *cans* and nuns or conical respectively, due to their shapes.

Different Rules for Different Places when inbound/returning

Maritime marks used to indicate the edge of a channel are distinguished by their color, being red or green, and shape. Two different schemes are in use worldwide, differing in their use of color. The International Association of Lighthouse Authorities defines them as System A and System B.

System A - Used by Europe, Australia, New Zealand, parts of Africa and most of Asia other than the Philippines, Japan and Korea.

Port marks are **red** and may have a red light.

Starboard marks are green and may have a green light.

System B - Used by North America, Central America and South America, the Philippines, Japan and Korea.

Port marks are green and may have a green light.

Starboard marks are red and may have a red light.

In both systems:

Port marks are square or have a flat top.

Starboard marks are conical (or present a triangular shape) or have a pointed top.

Day beacons are any of a wide variety of unlighted nautical sea marks. Typically, they're used to supplement lighted buoys in marking channels, but they may also mark smaller navigable routes in their entirety.

Light beacons are lighted nautical sea marks used for navigating after dark. While you find them commonly in well-populated, frequently used waterways, many don't have lit beacons of any kind.

Fog signals are devices used in fog to mark a hazard or a key navigation point, such as a shallow reef or a harbor entrance. Fog signals produce an audible warning and sometimes a visual one, too.

Lightships are vessels stationed offshore to warn other vessels of hazards to navigation. Besides lights, they are typically equipped with fog signals and radio beacons.

You can learn more about regional and international rules of the road and locally recognized navigational markings in the websites listed in the Popular Websites for Boating Laws & Regulations sidebar.

Dive flags. You're probably already familiar with the Alpha (blue and white) and diver-down (red with white stripe) flags. Depending upon where you are, your boat may be required to fly either or both flags when divers are in the water. The Alpha flag is an international boating signal that means "I have divers in the water and am restricted in my ability to maneuver." The red divers down flag means "I have divers in the water – keep clear a safe distance." The distance is commonly dictated by regulations, typically mandating that other vessels stay 30 to 90 metres/100 to 300 feet away. The flag flown and the distance to stay away are dictated by local regulations.

Navigational Charts and Instruments

Charts. Just as a street map graphically represents roads you would take when you drive, a nautical chart graphically represents a maritime area and adjacent coastal regions where a captain may operate a boat.

Unlike a typical road map, however, a nautical chart shows geographic features such as water depths, hazards, natural and artificial navigation aids, tide and current information, structures (harbors, buildings, bridges, etc.) and even local details about the earth's magnetic field (magnetic variation). You use navigational charts for navigation, but they're more like terrestrial topographic maps than like road maps. Charts (and instruments) are essential for safe navigation in many areas, yet almost never needed in others where vessels operate entirely within sight of land and tie up to established moorings. This is common at many popular dive destinations. However, local regulations may require a commercial vessel to carry charts and instruments either way.

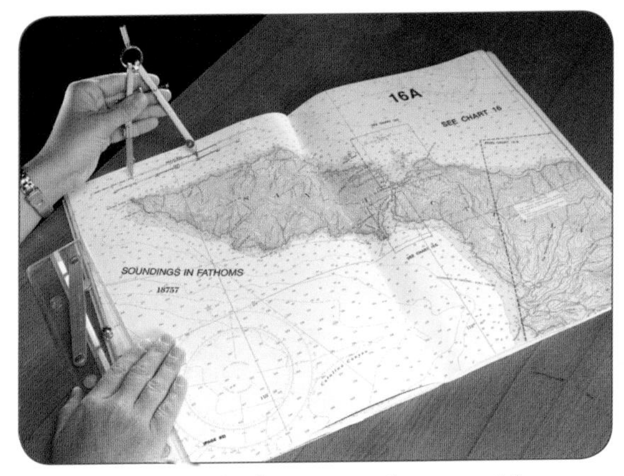

Navigational charts used in boating are similar to terrestrial topographic maps that show physical features.

Not all navigational charts are printed anymore. With the rise of GPS (Global Positioning System) navigation and other electronic instrumentation, captains increasingly opt for electronic charts integrated with other instruments because they provide the same information in a more versatile format. These charts display on a monitor, typically showing the boat's location, plotted courses and other information.

To provide compatibility between the government offices that create, maintain and update electronic charts and instrumentation, the charts follow a standardized Electronic Chart Display and Information System (ECDIS) format. As of July 2008, the use of this standard for all electronic navigational charts and electronic chart displays is international law.

Instruments. If you look in the wheelhouse, chances are you'll see several navigation instruments – though in some areas, all navigation is by piloting and the captain really doesn't need instruments at all (more about this later). Globally, however, the typical vessel usually has two or more of several instruments.

Automated Direction Finders (ADFs) find the direction to a radio source – a radio beacon sending out a signal from a known location. Because radio can travel long distances over the horizon, ADFs make particularly good ground-based navigation systems. A direction finder simply tells the captain the direction to the broadcast point. Although GPS (discussed next) have by far become the dominating navigation instrument, low cost ADF systems have created a comeback in their use, and they're especially handy in some areas.

GPS – Global Positioning System is by far the prevailing navigation system, not just on water, but everywhere on earth. You're probably familiar with it from its rising use in cell phones, computers, automobile navigation systems, emergency vehicle routing and more. GPS units have become so compact and inexpensive that you can carry one in your back pocket. Therefore, it's rare to see a boat without at least a basic one.

GPS works by finding direction based on signals transmitted by more than two dozen CPS satellites. The signals provide the receiver with relative position information so that you can tell your location within a few metres/feet, and speed and direction when in motion. GPS is the most common electronic instrument that integrates navigational charts, allowing you to see exactly where you are on the chart, track your movement and choose destinations to which the GPS will guide you.

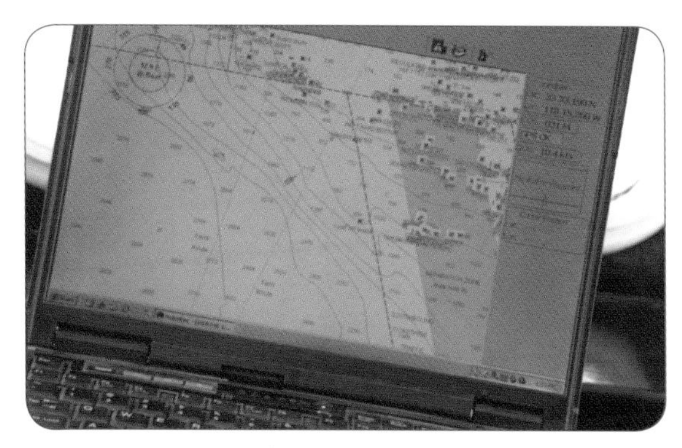

Boat GPS systems commonly integrate navigational charts, allowing you to see exactly where you are on the chart at any time.

Though you may not think of a *fathometer* as a navigational instrument, it actually is. A fathometer, (a.k.a. fishfinder or depthfinder, which differ slightly technically) is a specialized echo sounding system (active sonar) aimed toward the bottom. By using sonar echoes, you can determine the depth, find fish or even draw a picture of the bottom and the location of fish. Technically, a fathometer or depthfinder simply shows you depth as a digital display, whereas a fishfinder or "bottom machine" displays an image.

Because navigational charts show depth, knowing the depth helps the captain determine the vessel's position. In diving, the captain typically uses GPS or piloting to locate the dive site, then uses the fathometer (fishfinder) to pin point the best spot on the bottom. Another important use of fishfinders is finding *new* dive sites by cruising over potential areas. This is particularly true in locating wrecks.

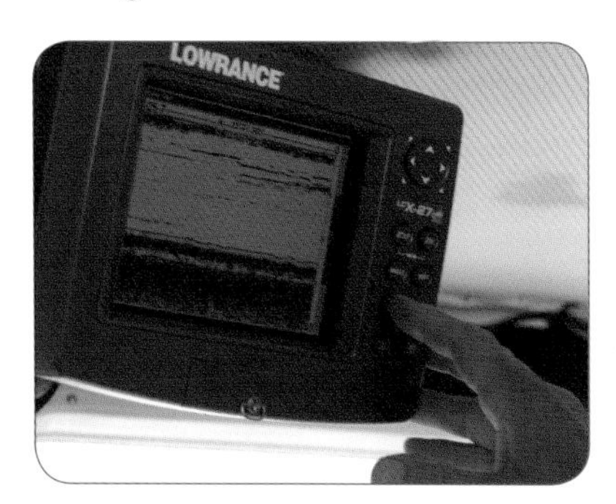

The fathometer or fishfinder provides depth information and allows the captain to see what the bottom looks like.

Today, fathometers/fishfinders often integrate with other instruments including GPS, electronic charts and even radar.

The earliest instrument sailors used was the compass, and it remains a primary tool for navigating in open water. Electronic compasses (often integrated with other instruments) are convenient and easy to read, especially when you're already referencing an electronic chart with GPS and depth information. However, conventional compasses remain popular and many boats have them in addition to electronic versions and GPS. Although some of this is likely due to tradition, a primary reason for this is that in the event of an onboard electrical problem, the compass continues to work even when all other instruments sputter out.

The conventional marine compass remains a popular instrument. This may be partly due to tradition, but also because in the event of an electrical failure, it still works when the sophisticated instrumentation is dead.

To learn more about compass use and navigation while diving, see the PADI *Underwater Navigator Manual* and *Underwater Navigation* video.

Docking and Undocking (Leaving the Dock)

As you may recall from the PADI Open Water Diver course and the PADI Rescue Diver course, the majority of dive accidents occur at the surface. This is the area where you transition from above water to underwater or vice versa, and the transition has some potential problems when divers don't follow proper procedures and adhere to good habits.

Docking and undocking are similar transitions in boating, going from a freely operating vessel to one tied in place or vice versa. And also similarly, you avoid problems by following procedures that take you smoothly through this transition.

⚠ On a charter dive boat, responsibility for docking and undocking lies with the crew. **Only attempt to assist if specifically asked to do so by the crew. Politely decline if you feel that you would be unable to assist adequately or safely**. And there's certainly nothing wrong with offering to help if you know what you're doing, you make the offer without distracting the crew from what they're doing, and you don't do anything unless they accept.

As a passenger, during docking/undocking stay clear of dock lines and the side of the boat that is or will be tied up. The crew may ask all passengers to sit down. Doing this increases visibility for them and minimizes confusion caused by you and others moving about. It also has the benefit of reducing your risk of falling if the boat bumps the dock harder than expected. When you sit, try to do so away from the exhaust because the engine will likely be running for several minutes before departure and after arrival.

The crew may ask passengers to sit down during docking and undocking. This provides better visibility and reduces confusion.

Undocking & Docking Crew Procedures

Undocking – wind or current pushing the boat away from the dock

1. Cast off lines and pull in fenders as the wind blows the boat away from the dock.
2. When clear and safely away from the dock and other boats, the captain shifts the engines to forward and departs at ideal speed.

Undocking – wind or current is pushing the boat toward the dock

1. Cast off all lines except an after bow spring line (line from bow to cleat on dock amidships). This keeps the boat from moving forward and allows the stern to pivot away from the dock.
2. The crew puts a fender forward to cushion the bow of the boat against the dock.
3. The captain turns the motor or rudder to the direction necessary to push the stern away from the dock and shifts the engine forward at idle speed.
4. The stern swings away from the dock. When clear of obstacles and traffic, the crew casts off the spring line. The boat backs away from the dock and when safe shifts into forward and idle (let the engine revolve slowly with throttle nearly closed) away from the dock.

Docking procedure – wind blowing toward the dock

1. Before approaching the dock, the crew ensures one end of the docking line is secured onboard and that fenders are ready. Captain reduces speed.
2. Captain brings boat parallel to the dock at about .3 metres/2 feet off. The wind blows the boat in.

Docking procedure – wind blowing away from the dock (outboard/inboard outboard engines)

1. Before approaching the dock, the crew ensures one end of the docking line is secured onboard and that fenders are ready.
2. The captain approaches the dock at a 20- to 30-degree angle. The crew passes a bow line ashore and secures it.
3. Captain turns so propeller is towards the dock and reverses engine. This brings the stern into the dock.
4. The crew can secure the boat with the stern line.

Docking procedure – wind blowing away from the dock (inboard engines)

1. Before approaching the dock, the crew ensures one end of the docking line is secured onboard and that fenders are ready.
2. The captain approaches the dock at a 20- to 30-degree angle. The crew passes a bow line ashore and secures it.
3. The crew attaches an after bow spring to keep the boat from moving forward.
4. With the engine idling forward, the captain turns the wheel away from the dock. Since the boat cannot move forward, and the rudder pushes the stern toward the dock while the crew secures the other lines.

⚠ Do not disembark after docking until cleared to do so by the crew. There's a difference between a boat being tied up and a boat being secured. Often the initial tie simply keeps the boat from drifting away from the dock, and it will take additional ties and adjustments before the vessel's secure enough for people to climb off and on.

⚠ **Another important point is that you should never use your feet or arms in an attempt to slow anything but a very small boat that appears it will strike the dock or other obstacle.** It's a common misperception that because a boat is moving slowly, it will be easy to stop. This isn't true, because the size of the boat is part of the equation. **Although the vessel may not be moving that fast, the momentum due to size can cause significant injuries, *especially* if your limbs get trapped between the vessel and the dock.** A large boat that is moving very slowly can still crush and/or break your arm or leg if it gets pinned between the boat and the dock. Leave it to the captain to use the engine to stop the boat.

Never use your feet or arms in an attempt to slow anything but a very small boat that appears it will strike the dock or other obstacle.

If you're assisting the crew (or helping out on a private boat) undock, keep in mind that the dock lines may stay with the boat, or they may stay on the dock. Follow the crew's directions regarding which end of the line to release – the end on the boat or the end on the dock.

When assisting with tie up, you always tie the line – whether on the boat or the dock – to a cleat. Never tie to the boat's rail or route the line so there's stress against anything other than the cleat, and never tie to anything but a cleat unless directed to do so by the crew.

When tying to the cleat, always run the line to the side of the cleat opposite the line's origination – remember *belay away*. Pass the line in a figure S and take up slack as directed by the crew. Secure the lie by passing it in a figure eight around the cleat twice, turning the last loop under on itself as shown in the photos. The turn-under causes the tie to tighten rather than loosen when the boat puts tension on the line. This is called a *cleat hitch*.

Always belay away. After using an S wrap to take up slack, secure the tie with two figure 8 wraps, turning the last loop under on itself so that tension from the boat makes the knot tighter.

Nautical Knots

There are five basic knots that every boater should know, some of which you may already know from the PADI Search and Recovery Diver course. Boaters favor knots that are easy to tie and then untie easily even after taking a tremendous amount of strain. However, it's important to use the correct knot for the application. Using the wrong knot can create a hazard, even if you tie it properly.

1. Cleat Hitch - Use this knot to secure the boat to a dock or secure a line to the boat you will probably use the cleat hitch. Take the line to the ear of the cleat furthest from where the line comes from (the load). Take one wrap around the base of the cleat and then start a figure eight across the top of the opposite ear. Finish with a half hitch turned under so that the line comes away from the cleat in the opposite direction from which it came in.

2. Bowline - Often called the "king" of knots, the bowline is very versatile. Use it to form a temporary loop that you can put over a piling or cleat, or to attach a line to an eye. The bowline won't slip or jam. Start by making an overhand loop that looks like a six. With the end of the line, come up through the hole in the six, around the back of the line you're holding and back down through the hole in the six. Grab the part of the line that went up through the hole and the part of the line that came back down through the hole in one hand, and the top of the line you were holding in the other, and pull taut.

3. Square knot (reef knot) - The square knot is used for lots of light duty including tying things down. Start with an overhand knot, like beginning to tie your shoe. Keeping the ends of the lines in your hand on the same side, cross them again and tie another overhand knot. If you don't keep them on the same side you'll end up with a granny knot that will jam.

The most important thing to remember about a square knot is to only use it for applications that have an even load pulling the line from both sides. Do not use it to create a loop or as a hitch, and do not use it when human safety or valuable cargo are involved. The square knot is primarily a convenience knot for tying things in place.

4. Round turn and two half hitches - Use this knot to tie to a piling, mooring or ring. Simply take a full turn around the object being tied to and take two half hitches around the line itself. Route the line over and up through, then under and down through.

5. Clove Hitch - This knot is handy to quickly tie to a piling, but do not leave it unattended or for long periods because it can come loose. You may add a couple of half hitches as above to make it more permanent. This knot is simply two loops with an end tucked under. For a more secure tie, use the round turn and two half hitches.

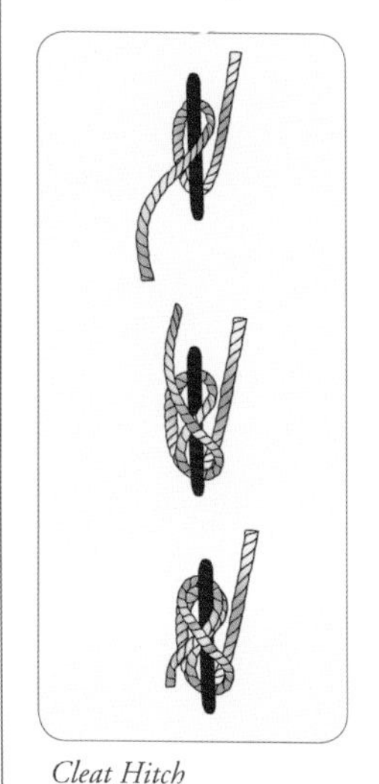

Cleat Hitch

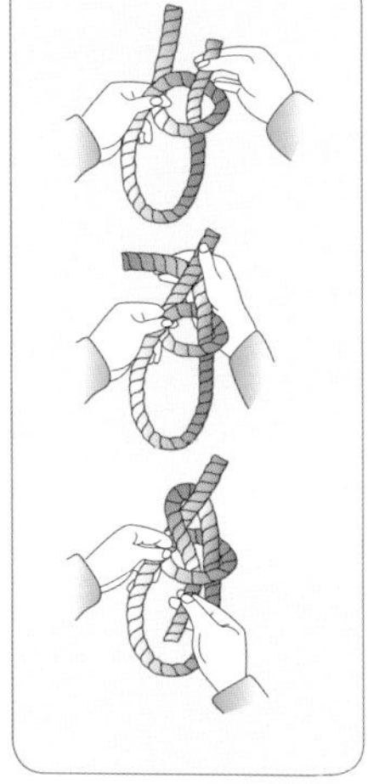

Bowline

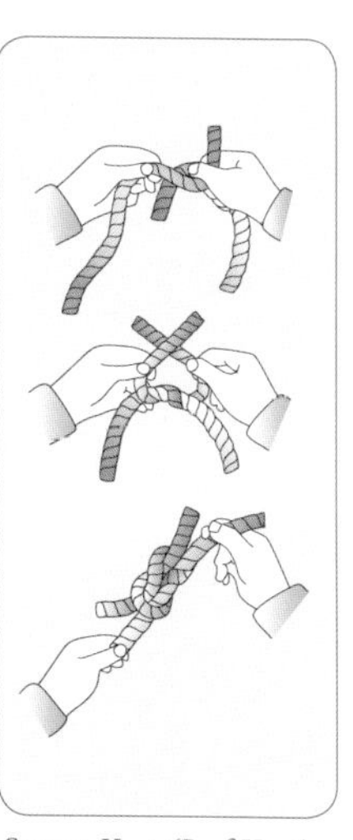

Square Knot (Reef Knot)

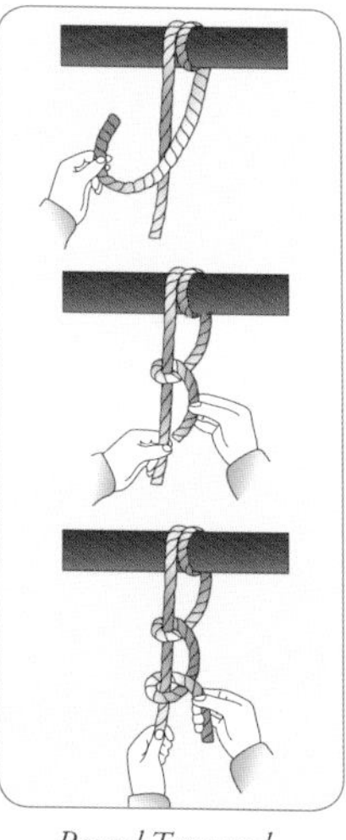

Round Turn and Two Half Hitches

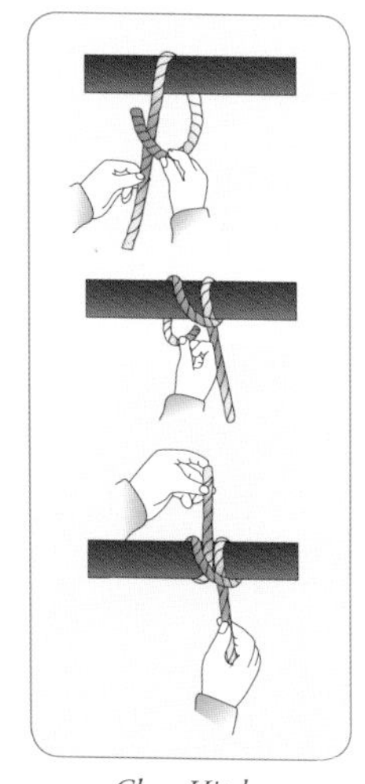

Clove Hitch

Exercise 4 - Boating Basics for Divers

1. When a vessel approaches your boat (not under sail) from the starboard
   - ☐ a. it makes way.
   - ☐ b. you have way.
   - ☐ c. There's not enough information to answer.

2. Local rules of the road are usually the same as international rules of the road.
   - ☐ True ☐ False

3. Common, local navigational aids include (check all that apply):
   - ☐ a. marine traffic signals.
   - ☐ b. buoys.
   - ☐ c. day beacons.
   - ☐ d. fog signals.

4. Navigational charts are similar to terrestrial ____________ maps.
   - ☐ a. road
   - ☐ b. topographic
   - ☐ c. population

5. Navigational instruments found on boats commonly include (check all that apply):
   - ☐ a. compass.
   - ☐ b. GPS.
   - ☐ c. ADF.
   - ☐ d. fathometer.

6. You're on a large charter boat that appears it will collide with the dock. You should
   - ☐ a. use your feet to stop the boat from striking.
   - ☐ b. keep your arms and legs clear so you're not injured.

How'd you do?

1. a. 2.True. 3. b, c, d. 4. b. 5. a, b, c, d. 6. b.

Boat Diving Safety/ *Emergency Equipment*

Study Objectives

Underline/highlight the answers to these questions as you read:

1. What eight pieces of basic safety equipment do you typically find on dive boats?
2. Where would you typically find each of those eight pieces of safety equipment?
3. How do you operate the marine radio on board a dive boat according to local regulations and procedures?

Safety/Emergency Equipment

Just as local laws and regulations stipulate local rules of the road, boat ownership requirements, and crew and captain qualifications, they stipulate minimums for safety equipment aboard a boat. Beyond that, a *dive* boat has equipment requirements that may not be required by law, but may be standard practice in the local dive community.

There are eight pieces of basic safety equipment that you'll typically find on dive boats. For legally required equipment, check with your local boat regulating agencies, such the websites listed earlier.

PFDs. (Personal Flotation Devices, a.k.a. life preservers). The most basic piece of boating safety gear is the PFD, which keeps you afloat if the boat sinks or capsizes, or if you must abandon ship due to fire.

Local regulations stipulate the number and type of PFDs required, but in most areas, the absolute minimum is one *wearable* PFD for each person on board. In addition, buoyant cushions, life rings and ring buoys are highly desirable, and in most areas at least one throwable flotation device is required on vessels longer than 5 metres/15 feet. Note that in most areas, your BCD does *not* qualify as a PFD.

Besides having wearable PFDs, everyone on board needs to know where to find them and how to use them. This is usually part of the crew briefing prior to departure, so be sure to listen. PFDs are typically stowed so they're out of the way, but must obviously be quickly accessible in an emergency. Most PFDs are easy to use, but the time to be figuring out how is not when you're about to step overboard!

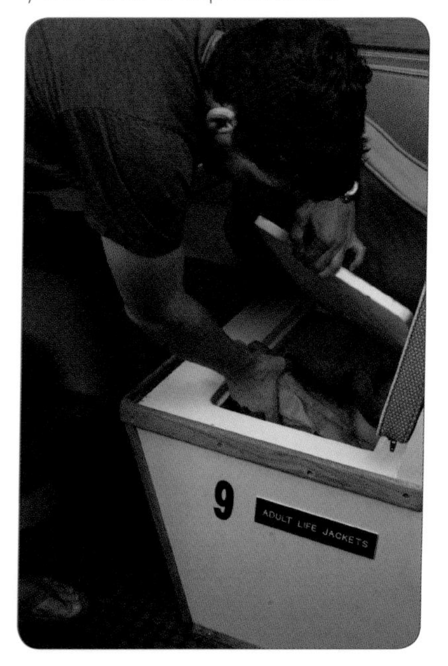

A boat should have at least one wearable PFD for each person on board. You should know where they are and how to use them.

Fire extinguishers. A boat is one of the worst places to have a fire for the simple reason that there's no place to run except over the side. This is why crews take fire safety (including restrictions on where and when you can and can't smoke) very seriously.

Despite this, not all vessels are required to carry fire extinguishers, but this is primarily because fire is highly unlikely on some boats. It would be unreasonable to require a fire extinguisher on a sea kayak or a sailboat that has neither an engine nor a generator. On the other hand, any vessel that has an engine and carries combustible fuel (i.e., the vast majority of boats you'd be diving from) should have at least one fire extinguisher.

Because a boat is made of solid combustibles, has flammable fuels and also has an electrical system, most boats carry A-B-C rated extinguishers. Fire extinguisher classifications may vary from country to country. These are the ones rated for all three types of fires. Fire extinguishers should be mounted in the open near likely fire areas (such as the engine), but far enough away that you can retrieve them safely. Fire extinguishers require periodic inspection and servicing, or replacement for the single-use type.

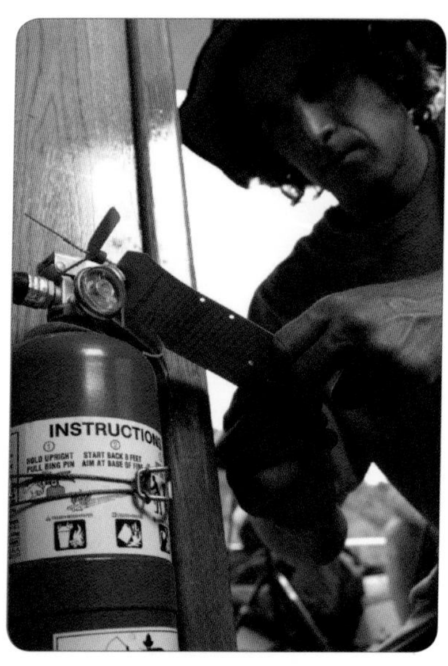

The recommended fire extinguishers for boats are those rated A-B-C. They should be mounted in the open near likely fire sources, but far enough away for safe retrieval.

In the event of a fire, it's useful to know the best way to use an extinguisher for the type of fire. For a solid combustible fire (fabric, cloth, wood, etc.), spray the extinguisher directly at the base of the fire. For fuels or liquids, surround and cover the flames, using the extinguisher to separate the fire from the fuel. In case of an electrical fire, disconnect the power. Although this stops the immediate cause of fire, you may still need the extinguisher because electrical fires often trigger combustible solids or fuel.

Sound signaling devices. On most larger vessels, this is the ship's horn. On small boats like inflatables, you may use a whistle, though there are horns as well. Sound signaling devices are important because they're required according to the rules of the road in given circumstances, as well as to alert other boats much as you do with an automobile horn.

Because they're used in navigation, horns are nearly always triggered from the wheelhouse or bridge – any place where there's a ship's wheel. On small boats, the whistle or other device stays within easy reach.

Visual distress signals. Local regulations commonly stipulate what types of visual distress signaling devices must be aboard. Typical ones include distress flares, smoke flares, meteor rockets, flare guns, distress lights and signal mirrors. They must be in serviceable condition (as in the case of flares, which have a marked service life). In many areas, vessels above a certain size must carry a minimum of three pyrotechnic (flare) devices.

Typically, visual distress signals are stored with emergency supplies, though some like lights are general-purpose tools as well and may be stowed elsewhere.

The Emergency Signal Mirror

In an emergency situation, what can you use if you can't find a "proper" signaling device? Check your computer case for a CD or the stack of DVDs. The silver side makes an effective mirror for emergency signaling, and you can use the center hole to aim it, just like you would with a "real" signal mirror.

Failing that, remember that anything bright and shiny will work if you have sunlight: a strip of aluminum foil, a piece of the mirror out of the head or a high polish piece of metal.

Bilge pump or bailer. All boats take on water as a normal part of operation. Not only does water come aboard due to waves and running off of wet divers, but it comes in small amounts through, for example, the propeller shaft through-hulling fitting with inboard engines. The worst case is when very rough water or a hole in the hull allows water to come in at a rate that could sink the boat.

All boats carry some kind of bilge pump or bailer, and again, local regulations may stipulate the number and type required. A small boat like an inflatable may require nothing more sophisticated than a small bucket, but larger vessels usually have electrical pumps and/or hand pumps.

You usually find the bilge pump switch near the wheel, and most larger vessels have automatic triggers that pump excess water when it rises to a certain level in the bilge. Most boats also have one or more manual bailing devices in case of a power failure, and in the case of a big leak, so that manual bailing can supplement the motorized pumping until emergency repairs are made. Portable bilge pumps and pails are usually kept with emergency supplies. Manual pumps that are installed are typically accessed below deck (near the keel where the water will be), and you may need to remove deck covers to reach them.

You usually find the bilge pump switch near the captain's station by the wheel.

First aid kit. Regulations usually require commercial vessels to have first aid kits, and it's a good idea for any dive boat, private or chartered. Most will have basic first aid supplies including bandages, dressings, tape, antiseptic ointments, sunburn lotions and water, with tools such as medical scissors and tweezers. Diver-specific items include having a pocket mask for rescue breathing, as well as vinegar, hot compresses and (in some regions) antivenin for marine life related injuries.

Most boats keep first aid supplies in a sealed, moisture proof plastic box either below deck or in the wheelhouse. On charter boats, the crew will usually tell you where to find first aid supplies during the boat briefing.

To learn more about first aid in diving and non-diving medical emergencies, see the PADI *Rescue Diver Manual*. It's recommended that you complete the PADI Rescue Diver, PADI Emergency Oxygen Provider and the Emergency First Response Primary Care (CPR) and Secondary Care (first aid) courses.

Oxygen equipment. Emergency oxygen has become the standard dive community practice for a diving emergency related to suspected decompression illness (DCI). This is not a boating regulation, but one specific to diving.

The recommended oxygen system for use by lay rescuers in diving emergencies is the non resuscitator demand-valve, which delivers 100 percent oxygen to the patient. The system should also have freeflow oxygen for aiding unresponsive or weak patients.

You'll typically find the oxygen system in a sealed plastic box (usually green or orange) with other emergency and first aid supplies. In situations involving very close to shore in very small, wet boats (e.g. sea kayaks), both oxygen and first aid are not kept aboard (no room and would quickly suffer water damage) but at a nearby, quickly accessible shore location.

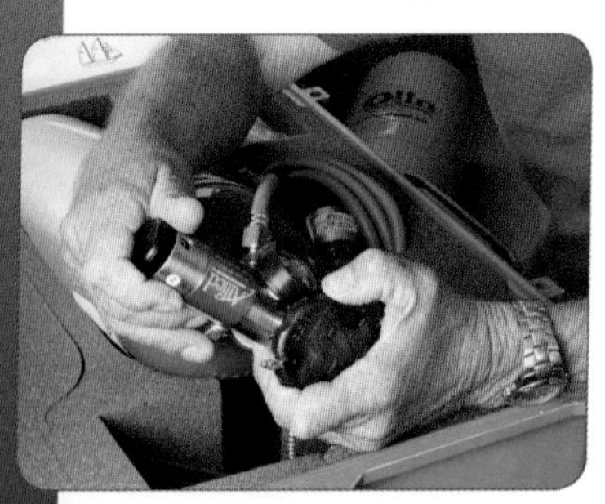

You'll typically find the emergency oxygen stored some place safe and dry with other emergency equipment.

To learn more about oxygen equipment for diver emergencies and its use, see your PADI Instructor about enrolling in the PADI Rescue Diver course.

Marine radio. Most vessels larger than a runabout or kayak will have a marine radio. Vessels beyond a certain size (usually 3-5 metres/10-15 feet) are required to have a marine radio in most jurisdictions. The captain uses a marine radio for routine communications as well as emergencies.

Before using a marine radio in an emergency, it's important to know what qualifies as an emergency: a situation in which you or your vessel is threatened by grave danger that may cause severe injury or loss of life. Running out of fuel, a dead battery or another mechanical problem is *not* an emergency (the captain may request aid via a marine radio, but using routine communications, not the emergency protocols). Since it's used in routine navigation, you nearly always find the marine radio near the ship's wheel.

Local areas may designate specific frequencies (channels) for different purposes, but in most areas, Channel 16 is used as the hailing and emergency channel. You never hold a conversation on 16, but use it to contact another party and then switch to another channel for the conversation.

A call of pan-pan means that there is an emergency on board but that, for the time being at least, there is no immediate danger to anyone's life or to the vessel itself. This is distinct from a Mayday call, which means there is imminent danger to life or to the continued viability of the vessel itself. In the event of an emergency, go to Channel 16 and say, "Mayday, mayday, mayday. This is (repeat the vessel's name three times). My position is (give latitude/longitude or bearing from a known point – don't guess if unsure). I have (state type) emergency. Over." Listen for Coast Guard or similar authority or nearby vessels to reply. If you hear nothing, repeat the distress call. Be prepared to give more information such as vessel description, location details, more about the emergency, equipment you have available and so on.

If you have trouble reaching anyone by radio, try your cell phone if you're not far from shore. In some areas, authorities receive more vessel distress calls by cell phone than by radio.

Boat Diving Plan

Although regulations do not require a boat diving plan, it's a good idea to prepare one before undocking and leaving it with someone responsible. Many charter vessels do this as a matter of routine (especially those operating from a dive center or resort and following a daily schedule), and it's a wise practice for private boaters.

The plan should outline your planned itinerary, including when you plan to depart, where you're going, the route you'll follow, when you plan to be back, and at what time someone should consider you overdue and contact authorities. It should also describe your boat, and list the number of people aboard. If you'll be within a cell coverage area, put your phone number on it as well.

Exercise 5 - Boat Diving Safety/Emergency Equipment

1. The eight pieces of safety equipment you typically find on dive boats include (check all that apply):
   - ☐ a. emergency oxygen.
   - ☐ b. visual signaling devices.
   - ☐ c. marine radio.
   - ☐ d. sound signaling devices.
   - ☐ e. first aid kit.
   - ☐ f. PFDs
   - ☐ g. bilge pump or bailer.
   - ☐ h. fire extinguisher.

2. Running out of fuel or a mechanical problem is __________ an emergency according to marine radio protocols.
   - ☐ a. never
   - ☐ b. always
   - ☐ c. usually
   - ☐ d. frequently

How'd you do?

1. a, b, c, d, e, f, g, h. 2. a.

Basic Guides to *Boating and Safety*

Study Objectives

Underline/highlight the answers to these questions as you read:

1. What does the term *piloting* mean?
2. What are the seven dimensions of piloting?
3. What does the term *dead reckoning* mean, and how do you use the basic principles of dead reckoning while piloting a boat?
4. What are four considerations when selecting a mooring or an anchorage for diving?
5. How do you tie up to and release from a mooring?
6. How do you set up, secure, deploy retrieve, and stow an anchor on board a dive boat?
7. What are the basic guides to boating safety?

Piloting

Words like "piloting," "navigating," "steering" and so on tend to get used interchangeably, and most of the time, what we mean is clear. However, sometimes these terms have very specific meanings for a particular way of operating a vessel. In this respect, *piloting* means to use landmarks, aids to navigation and soundings to guide a boat safely through channels, harbors and along coasts where dangers to navigation require your constant attention to position and course. In other words, it's finding your way based on what you see around the boat. This separates piloting from open ocean operations during which a captain may use GPS and compass headings for navigation.

All vessels must be piloted at various times. In some areas, virtually all boat operation takes place based on piloting, whereas other vessels (particularly transoceanic ships) only use piloting for approaching and leaving port. Piloting has seven dimensions: direction, distance, time, speed, position, depth and height.

Direction refers to the position of one point relative to another, usually between where you are and another point, or between two known points when you're navigating. *Distance* is the space between two points, which the pilot my judge based on linear measurement (metres/feet/nautical miles) or based on *time*, i.e., how long it takes to get from one point to another at a given speed. A pilot doesn't need as accurate time keeping as does say, a celestial navigator, but the ability to roughly determine time is important in piloting. *Speed* is how fast the vessel's going, as well as estimates of other vessels, the pilot must constantly be aware of the boat's position. *Depth* is measured either directly with a depth finder (fathometer), or indirectly based on the boat's position compared to experience with the local waters, charts and channel markings. *Height* is primarily a concern for sailing vessels, but applies to any vessel with a mast that must pass under a bridge or other low obstacles.

Dead Reckoning (DR)

Before the invention of GPS, the primary means of navigation when well beyond sight of land was *dead reckoning*. Dead reckoning is determining the boat's position based on estimated changes from its last determined position by tracking the courses steered and speeds. In other words, it's a highly educated (and with experience surprisingly accurate) guess.

With the rise of GPS, dead reckoning isn't nearly as common as it once was, but it's still taught as a means of navigating in the case GPS and other means of navigation should fail. And, like many esoteric skills, some captains carry it on because they enjoy the challenge and skill it requires, and they don't want to see it become a lost art.

To dead reckon, the captain needs to track the vessel's course, the heading (which isn't always the same as the course due to wind and current), speed and distance – the intended future path for the boat. The track always starts from a known position. Then, the captain or navigator plots the boat's course estimate on a chart, updating it frequently based upon changes in heading, speed or other variables. The course is updated and dead reckoning restarts upon reaching a known navigation point, such as a recognizable landmark. As you may imagine, prior to modern electronic navigation, the captain navigated by combining dead reckoning with piloting and, when the sky was clear, celestial navigation (use of the stars and sun to determine position).

Mooring and Anchoring

The vast majority of boat diving takes place with the vessel moored or anchored over or near the dive site. To those who watch the process, it looks deceptively simple. Tie up to a mooring ball or throw an anchor over the side and let out some line – what more could there be to it? The answer is, "more than you might imagine."

Although you probably know this, for clarity let's define *mooring* and *anchoring*. Mooring means you secure the boat over a site by tying to a permanently placed anchor system called (not surprisingly) a mooring. With a mooring, a buoyed line to the bottom remains permanently in place, and the boat ties to the line. Anchoring means you secure the boat over a site by dropping anchor.

Mooring *means you secure the boat over a site by tying to a permanently placed anchor system called a mooring.*

Anchoring *means you secure the boat over a site by dropping anchor.*

Of the two systems, moorings are preferred and have become common at dive sites at popular dive destinations. However, in areas where environmental or management consideration limit the use of moorings, responsible anchoring is a prevailing practice. Moorings make it easier to find the dive site, to secure the boat and to reduce environmental damage. Anchors are still commonly used by dive boats in places with resilient environments that can withstand anchoring without a significant environmental effect. In many of these places, the environment is such that moorings aren't practical because storms and high seas destroy them.

Whether mooring or anchoring, the captain has four considerations when securing the boat for diving. The first of these is *proximity to the dive site*. While it's not always possible, the ideal spot is directly over the dive site or immediately next to it, or in the middle of it if it's a very large site. The idea is to avoid a long air-wasting swim and to make it easy for divers to find the site. A second consideration is *diver safety*. Sometimes a dive site may be inappropriate due to boat traffic, current, waves or other conditions. Similarly, a third consideration is *boating safety*. The mooring/anchor site may be fine for divers, but, for example, a wind shift could swing the boat into some rocks. Finally, *conditions* are an issue, just as they are at any dive site. There's not much point in diving if there's no visibility, even if you have a perfectly safe anchorage directly over a dive site.

Mooring setup and mooring. Mooring is simpler and quicker than anchoring, it still has considerations and procedures. The vessel must be equipped for mooring prior to setting out, and different mooring systems have varying requirements. We'll look at a common mooring system setup and its procedures, but it's important to be familiar with the specifics of a mooring you plan to use.

For "typical" moorings, the crew prepares a short line (3-5 metres/10-15 feet) with a quick shackle on the free end. The line routes through the anchor tackle and secures on the anchor cleat with a cleat hitch. There is a boat hook stored on the bow, or place where someone can pass it easily to a crewmember on the bow.

Set up for a typical mooring includes a 3-5 metre/10-15 foot line with a quick shackle, secured to the anchor cleat and routed through the anchor tackle.

As with anchoring, the captain ensures the area is clear of divers and boats while approaching and motoring gently toward the mooring buoy. Using the boat hook, someone on the bow pulls aboard the line trailing from the buoy, passing it under the rail. The crewmember snaps and secures the shackle to the eye in the trailing line, ensuring that when the line's released, it will put tension only on the anchor tackle and cleat.

After securing the line, the end is cast off while the captain puts the engine in neutral, allowing the boat to drift back to confirm its holding before shutting down. Moorings are well secured and have adequate line or *scope* coming up, so there's no need for additional scope. The short scope is an advantage for you during the dive because you reach the bottom faster following it down. The drawback compared to anchor line is that when mooring lines are not changed frequently, they are quickly overgrown by a variety of organisms, so you may have to wear gloves and watch where you put your hands. However, if you dive in an area where wearing gloves is prohibited, take off your gloves as soon as you clear the line and secure them in your BCD pocket until you need them for ascent.

Releasing from a mooring. After all divers are aboard and accounted for, the captain makes sure the area is clear of boats, divers, etc. and starts the engine. The captain motors gently toward the mooring while the crew pulls in line, releases the shackle, and casts loose. The captain allows the boat to drift away from the mooring buoy before engaging the engine to avoid accidentally entangling the line in the propeller.

Note: In many dive destinations, particularly those with fragile reefs and/or vulnerable shipwrecks, mooring systems are increasingly becoming the rule. To learn more and to become involved in local mooring buoy projects visit the Project AWARE website and download the *Mooring Buoy Planning Guide* from http://www.projectaware.org.

Anchor set up and anchoring. Anchoring begins long before you leave the dock by having your anchor set up and ready. That means having the correct type of anchor for the bottom you'll be placing it in, such as a Danforth® anchor for sand or a grappling hook for rocky bottoms. The lower portion (usually 3-6 metres/10-20 feet) of the anchor line is chain to resist abrasion and to aid the anchor's grip. The anchor line and chain feed off the bow from the anchoring tackle, with the line stowed in the chain locker so it deploys without resistance when you drop anchor.

Anchoring begins with anchor set up, which includes having the right anchor type and routing the line and chain from the chain locker through the boat's anchoring tackle.

To anchor, the captain motors over the anchor spot and heads into wind so the anchor is less likely to disturb the bottom (found via piloting, GPS and the fishfinder). After checking that the area is clear of divers, boats, sensitive organisms or cultural artifacts, the captain maintains the boat in position while the anchor is released so it drops to the bottom. When it makes contact, the captain puts the boat in neutral and allows it to drift back while paying out anchor line.

The amount of line released depends upon the bottom type, the boat and anchor sizes and the wind/current pushing the boat. The more line or scope, the better the anchor holds all else being equal. For short-term anchorages in calm conditions, the recommendation is that the scope should be at least three times the depth, For longer stays or depending on the situation, the crew may use more scope.

With sufficient scope released, the crew ties off the anchor line on the anchor cleat. The captain makes sure that the anchor is secure (not dragging) before shutting down the engine. Someone should check periodically to be sure the anchor continues to hold.

The longer the scope, the better the anchor grips. For short-term stays in calm conditions, a scope at least three times the depth is usually recommended.

Ensure that the anchor line has a quick release shackle and buoy attached so you can jettison the anchor in an emergency without having to retrieve it from the bottom.

Note that in some areas with sensitive aquatic life or vulnerable cultural artifacts, it is illegal to anchor except in a life-threatening emergency. Such areas will have moorings if diving is permitted.

Weighing anchor (anchor retrieval). When it's time to go, the captain and crew confirm that all divers are aboard and the area around the boat is clear of hazards such as other boats and their divers. The captain starts the engine and motors toward the anchor while taking up and stowing anchor line. When nearly directly over the anchor, the anchor will no longer hold well and be easy to pull from the bottom. If the boat is a small boat with a small anchor, one or two people simply haul the anchor up, hand over hand. Large boats (such as the typical dive charter boat) use the anchor winch to raise the anchor. To minimize damage to the environment, the captain motors in place until the anchor comes well clear of the bottom.

Basic Guides to Boating Safety

As with dive safety, boat safety is more a matter of attending to many small things than one big thing. In the excitement of heading out on a boat dive, if you're on a private vessel, it's possible to overlook something that prevents boat emergencies or allows you to respond to emergencies effectively.

Just as you learned to perform a predive safety check to make sure you're not overlooking the basics, boaters run through a quick predeparture checklist and to abide by the following basic guides to boating safety. The captain and crew are responsible for most of the following guides when you dive from a charter boat. When you dive from your own vessel, these are *your* responsibilities.

- Have the safety equipment you learned about earlier and know how to use it.
- Maintain the boat and its equipment in top working order.
- Know and obey the rules of the road.
- Operate your vessel with care, courtesy, and common sense towards other boaters and the environment.
- Always keep your boat under complete control.
- Watch posted speeds. Slow down in anchorages.
- Never overload your vessel. Stay within the rated capacity and loading requirements.
- Keep lifesaving equipment (PFDs, first aid, oxygen, fire extinguishers) accessible.
- Check local weather reports and sea condition reports before departure.
- Inspect the hull, engine, and all gear frequently.
- Keep the bilges clean and electrical contacts tight.
- Guard rigidly against any fuel system leakage.
- Keep fire extinguishers instantly available.
- Take maximum precautions to prevent fire while fueling.
- Use adequate scope when anchoring.
- Where available, request and meet the requirements for voluntary marine safety inspection certification (such as the U.S. Coast Guard Auxiliary Courtesy Marine Examination). These usually have higher requirements than the legal minimums.
- Complete a boating class. Do not operate a vessel beyond your abilities or the limits of your licensed rating.

In Case of an Accident

Fortunately, boat accidents are rare. However, should you be involved in an incident on a vessel when an injury requiring medical treatment, the disappearance of someone, significant property damage or a fatality occurs, an incident report must be filed with responsible law enforcement agencies in most areas. This is normally the responsibility of the captain and/or vessel owner.

In the event of an incident, all vessels involved are required to stop and provide assistance to other persons as needed regardless of which vessel they're on, provided doing so doesn't endanger a boat providing aid, passengers or crew. In some countries, all vessels – involved in the incident or not – are required to provide assistance if they can do so without endangering themselves. Failure to provide aid when legally required to do so can carry stiff penalties. (Fortunately, most boaters and divers would do this anyway.) Sometimes local authorities request vessels in the area to assist.

If you're captaining a private vessel or aboard a chartered vessel that is assisting others, be prepared to help, but don't take unnecessary risks. This is like the PADI Rescue Diver philosophy that to be able to help, you have to keep yourself out of trouble first.

If your vessel is involved in an accident that includes damage to the fragile natural or cultural resources (such as groundings or spills), you should also contact local authorities, in particular when operating in environmentally sensitive areas such as marine parks and other protected sites. It is particularly important that you minimize the extent of damage already done and do not try to power off the damaged area. Instead, communicate with the authorities and wait for help.

Exercise 6 - Basic Guides to Boating and Safety

1. Piloting means
   - ☐ a. navigation with electronic instruments.
   - ☐ b. navigation based on what you see.
   - ☐ c. navigation based on your estimate from the boat's heading and speed.
2. The dimensions of piloting include (check all that apply):
   - ☐ a. direction.
   - ☐ b. distance.
   - ☐ c. GPS.
   - ☐ d. speed.
3. Dead reckoning means
   - ☐ a. navigation with electronic instruments.
   - ☐ b. navigation based on what you see.
   - ☐ c. navigation based on your estimate from the boat's heading and speed.
4. Considerations for selecting an anchorage or mooring include (check all that apply):
   - ☐ a. proximity to the dive site.
   - ☐ b. diver safety.
   - ☐ c. boat safety.
   - ☐ d. conditions.
5. When releasing from a mooring, the captain allows the boat to drift away from the mooring before engaging the engine.
   ☐ True ☐ False
6. When anchoring, the captain backs the boat up under power to set the anchor.
   ☐ True ☐ False
7. Basic safe boating guides include (check all that apply):
   - ☐ a. checking weather/sea conditions before departure.
   - ☐ b. inspecting the hull, engine and gear frequently.
   - ☐ c. keeping the bilges clean.
   - ☐ d. using adequate scope when anchoring.
   - ☐ e. operating your vessel with care, courtesy, and common sense towards other boaters and the environment.

How'd you do?
1. *b.* **2.** *a, b, d.* **3.** *c.* **4.** *a, b, c, d.* **5.** *True* **6.** *False. The boat is allowed to drift back and the anchor sets itself.* **7.** *a, b, c, d, e.*

Boat Diving *Preparation*

> **Study Objectives**
>
> Underline/highlight the answers to these questions as you read:
>
> 1. How do you prepare your equipment for a boat dive?
> 2. How do you prepare yourself for a boat dive?
> 3. How do you prevent seasickness?
> 4. What should you do if you get seasick?

Let's turn our attention from boating itself to your likely primary interest, *diving* from a boat. Even if you've been boat diving before – perhaps many times – it's worth covering the procedures in detail from beginning to end. Boat diving actually begins well before you arrive at the dock with the way you prepare, which differs in some respects from how you prepare for shore dives.

Preparing Your Gear

In many places where you might dive from shore, if you forget a piece of gear or it malfunctions, it's inconvenient, but you can quickly run to a local dive center, to the hotel or even home to buy, rent or otherwise replace it. This is seldom true on a boat. Most of the time, if you didn't bring it or it doesn't work, you do without – even missing the dives in the worst case.

Begin preparing your gear for a boat dive at least a few days in advance, if you can. This gives you time to repair, rent or replace anything that's missing or broken. Use an equipment checklist (there's one in the back of the PADI *Open Water Diver Manual*) to be sure you have everything, and inspect everything closely – especially if you've not used it in awhile. Check for worn mask and fins straps that may fail, test breathe your regulator and try out the zippers on your exposure suits.

Begin preparing your gear for a boat dive at least a few days in advance. Use a checklist to be sure you have everything, and inspect it for proper operation and wear.

If you've not done so already, be sure to mark your equipment so that you can tell yours from someone else's. It's not unusual for fins and other gear to jumble together after a dive, and marking your equipment reduces confusion. You can normally mark items where you can see your initials (or name) when you're not wearing them, but they're hidden when you are (underwater photographers you pose for will appreciate this), such as inside your fin pockets. Many dive boats provide cylinders, but if you'll be bringing your own, have it filled.

When you pack your gear bag, put everything in it in reverse from the order you'll need it, so what you need first is on top. This allows you to work directly from the bag without having to spread gear all over the deck. Normally, this means putting your fins in first, and your BCD and regulator in last because you take them out first to set up your gear. Of course, don't put weights or your cylinder in your gear bag. After diving your gear bag will be wet inside, so you probably want a separate bag for your log book, certification card, food, dry clothes, towel and other personal items you want to keep dry. A dry bag works well for this. Don't forget any legal documents if you'll need them, such as a fishing license, visas, passports, etc.

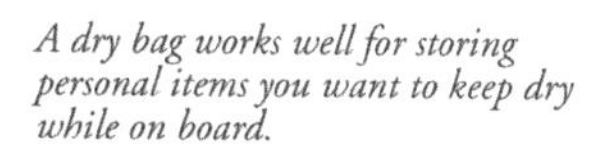

A dry bag works well for storing personal items you want to keep dry while on board.

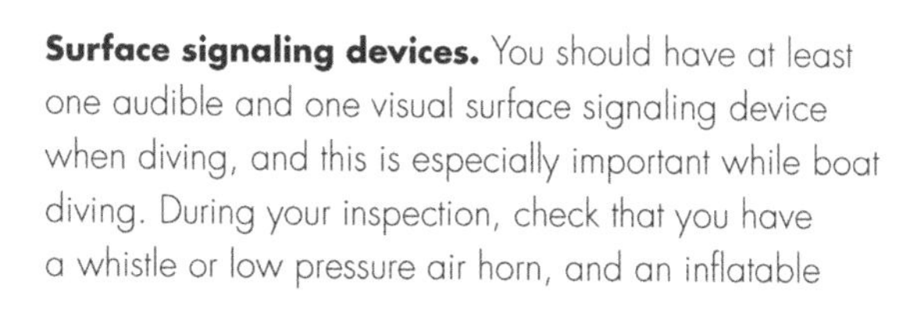

Surface signaling devices. You should have at least one audible and one visual surface signaling device when diving, and this is especially important while boat diving. During your inspection, check that you have a whistle or low pressure air horn, and an inflatable signal tube, flare or signal mirror in your kit. Most divers store these permanently in their BCDs so they know they always have them.

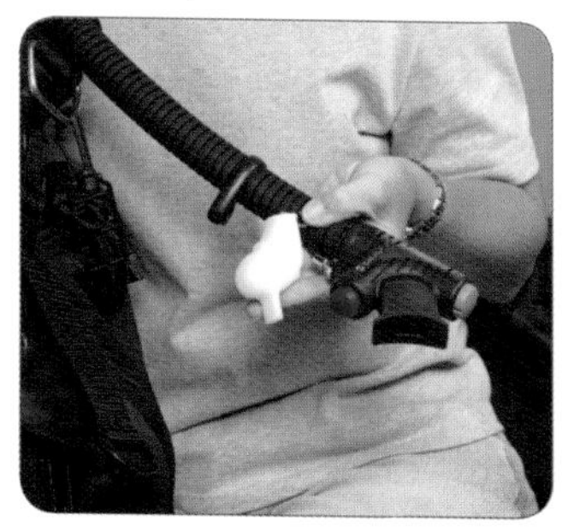

You should have at least one audible and one visual surface signaling device when diving.

Spare parts kit. If you want to avoid missing dives, you want a spare parts kit. You can buy prepackaged save-a-dive kits, which are a good start, but chances are you'll have to expand and customize yours with spares that fit your specific equipment. It also helps, by the way, to have spares for other divers because often, if your friends can't dive, you miss the dive, too, because you don't have a buddy.

Start with an appropriate container. A plastic tool box or fishing tackle box works well, though a water tight plastic case protects everything better if it can get very wet (like when diving from some small boats). You can keep both your spare parts and some basic tools in it. At a minimum, having the following in it:

- O-rings for different cylinder valves and DIN regulators
- Spare mask & fin straps
- Spare snorkel keeper
- Regulator mouthpiece with pull ties
- Various clips
- Adjustable wrench
- Allen wrench
- Scissors
- Wire cutters/point nose pliers
- Screw drivers (flat and Phillips)

Be sure to choose a box somewhat larger than you need at first, because your spare parts kit will grow as you add to it. Here's a tip: A good spare mask strap to carry is the neoprene/fabric type with Velcro™ type fasteners. These make good spares because they go on quickly and they fit almost any mask. Because these straps are self-securing, they will frequently work even when the mask buckle is broken.

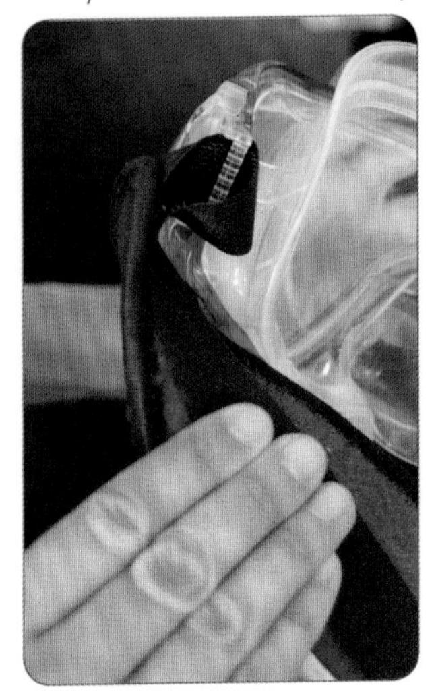

A good spare mask strap to carry is the neoprene/fabric type with Velcro™ type fasteners. They go on easily and fit almost any mask.

Preparing Yourself

Being out on a boat all day can present some physical demands that you want to prepare yourself for so you have an enjoyable experience. The night before, refrain from alcoholic beverages (a glass of wine or two isn't likely an issue, but be conservative) but drink plenty of fluids so you're well hydrated. Get enough sleep so you're well rested, and eat a healthful, well balanced meal. If appropriate, take any seasickness medications following your physician's or the product's guidelines (see the printed directions).

It may sound obvious, but the day before is a good time to think about how to get to the boat the next day: directions, boat name, charter fees, extra charges, etc. It's somewhat comical, but sometimes divers get up for a boat dive they booked through their local PADI Dive Center, only to realize they don't know where to go. Making sure you have all this information ahead of time spares you a last minute scramble with your telephone or surfing the internet when you want to be on your way.

Seasickness. Part of preparing yourself is planning for seasickness, or more properly, planning to *prevent* seasickness. Although seasickness is rarely serious or injurious in the long term, it is very unpleasant and can completely ruin a day of diving if you let it.

Seasickness (*motion* sickness, to be more accurate) is thought to be caused by an unusual disturbance of your vestibular (balance) system in your inner ear, coupled with conflicting perceptions between what your inner ear feels and what your eyes see. Physiologists still don't fully understand all the internal mechanisms that cause it, but they do know that people without a functioning vestibular system are immune. People have a wide range of susceptibility, you're most susceptible between ages 3 and 12, and women more are susceptible than men. Psychological and physiological conditions also contribute: fear, some drugs, being over heated, poor ventilation, smoke, exhaust, carbon monoxide, pregnancy, menstruation and performing intricate tasks (reading, sewing, repairing a regulator etc.). Some people adapt to motion after two or three days and will resist getting sick if not become entirely immune (you lose the adaptation after two or three days without motion, unfortunately).

The most effective way to prevent seasickness is to take a seasickness medication. You can find several brands available over the counter in most countries, though it's wise to consult with your physician. This is especially true if you take other medications. Whatever type you and your physician choose, read all warnings associated with it and follow the printed directions or the directions of your physician if different. Generally, you take medication well in advance of boarding so you *prevent* seasickness. Once you become seasick, medication seldom helps.

Besides taking medication, you can reduce the chances of getting seasick by avoiding greasy foods before boarding. Stay on deck, or at least in the fresh air, as close to the center of the boat as possible (it has the least motion). Look at something stationary on the horizon, and try to stay busy while avoiding intricate tasks. Get your gear set up so you can enter the water as soon as possible when you arrive at the dive site (though if you're very ill, you probably shouldn't dive).

Avoid breathing engine exhaust and avoid using the heads during rough weather. If you're taking an overnight trip, try to get a bunk as near the middle of the boat as you can.

To avoid seasickness, use seasickness medication, avoid greasy foods and don't breathe engine exhaust. Stay on deck in the fresh air, as near the center of the boat as possible.

If you do get sick, take heart. As unpleasant as the experience may be, you'll probably be fine as soon as you get ashore. In some areas, the seas at the dive site are much calmer than the seas in route, so you may feel much better as soon as the boat tucks into the lee of an island or reef (but this isn't always the case, unfortunately).

⚠ When sick, stay out of the boat's head. These small, cramped compartments will only make you feel worse. If you think you're going to vomit, go to the lee side (downwind) rail to do so. **Don't go alone (especially at night)**. Have someone come with you to be sure you don't go over the side while sick. After throwing up, try to drink some water (room temperature is usually best) to avoid dehydrating.

When you reach the dive site, if you're not feeling well, you may not be sure whether to go diving or not. If you do, you usually feel better underwater, though you may feel worse at the surface in the waves. And, you don't want to throw up underwater. If you're very sure you won't vomit in the water (perhaps only feeling mildly queasy), then diving may be fine and you'll probably feel better, at least until you come back aboard. If you may be sick enough to throw up, the prudent call is to stay on the boat.

Exercise 7 - Boat Diving Preparation

1. To prepare your gear for boat diving (check all that apply):
   - ☐ a. inspect everything a few days in advance.
   - ☐ b. make sure everything is marked.
   - ☐ c. pack your bag in the reverse order that you'll need everything.
   - ☐ d. make sure you have surface signaling devices.
2. To prepare yourself for a boat dive (check all that apply):
   - ☐ a. get enough sleep the night before.
   - ☐ b. be well hydrated.
   - ☐ c. have directions to the boat ahead of time.
   - ☐ d. eat a balanced meal.
3. To prevent seasickness (check all that apply):
   - ☐ a. use seasickness medication.
   - ☐ b. stay out of the boat's exhaust.
   - ☐ c. avoid intricate tasks.
   - ☐ d. stay busy.
4. If you get seasick, you should (check all that apply):
   - ☐ a. go into the head.
   - ☐ b. go to the windward rail to vomit.
   - ☐ c. avoid drinking water.
   - ☐ d. keep everyone away from you.

How'd you do?
1. *a, b, c, d.* **2.** *a, b, c, d.* **3** *a, b, c, d.* **4.** *None of the answers apply.*

Charter Boat Boarding and *Predive Procedures*

Study Objectives

Underline/highlight the answers to these questions as you read:

1. What are the general boarding procedures for a charter dive boat?
2. What four topics will a boat dive area orientation briefing usually cover?
3. What is the procedure for suiting up and gearing up on a dive boat?
4. Why is a predive roll call by divemasters or crewmembers important?

As you visit different dive destinations around the world, you'll find that each region's dive boats have somewhat differing protocols to follow when you come aboard. Since these protocols vary depending upon the type of boat, regional logistics, number of passengers and other differences between vessels, it is important that you always listen carefully to the briefing prior to diving. Nonetheless, the procedures you follow are outlined below.

Arrival and Boarding

As a rule of thumb, plan to arrive at the dive boat at least a half an hour prior to departure – or earlier if so requested by the crew. Make sure the crew's ready for you to board (they may still be preparing and need you to stay on the dock), and stow your gear according to their directions. This is important because there may be specific areas that need to be kept clear for safety or access, and certain areas may not be appropriate for lead or cylinders.

Generally, you'll stow personal items that you want to keep dry somewhere forward under cover. It's best to expect anything left on deck to get wet. The smaller the boat and the rougher the conditions, the more likely this is true. For small boats like inflatables that may not have reliably dry areas, a dry bag is a good option.

Most charter boats will have you fill your name in on a roster, plus complete paperwork such as liability releases/assumption of risk. It's important to complete these before the boat departs.

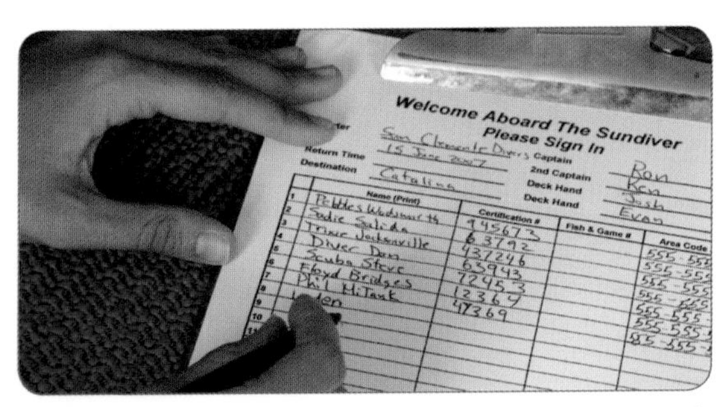

Be sure to put your name on the boat roster and complete any required paperwork before departure.

On some boats, you use any filled cylinder available, on some you bring your own and on yet others, you'll put your name on a specific cylinder. Follow the crew's direction, and again, be sure the cylinder is well secured in its rack, with the retaining bungee (if there is one) in place.

Predeparture and Predive Briefings

The captain, crew or divemaster will usually conduct a predeparture briefing, which may be separate from or include the predive briefing (typically depending upon how long the ride is to the site). Predeparture briefings and predive briefings are for your safety as well as enjoyment, so stop what you're doing and pay attention (besides, this is just common courtesy).

The predeparture briefing covers where to find safety equipment (PFDs, first aid, etc.) and a roll call from the roster to be sure it lists everyone aboard. Since the crew uses the roster to account for everyone, never answer for someone else, even if you believe that person is aboard. If you don't hear your name called, be sure to alert the divemaster/crew.

Most charter boats conduct a predeparture briefing, which may include a predive briefing. These briefings are for your safety and so you have fun, so stop what you're doing and listen.

The predeparture and/or predive briefing provides a boat dive area orientation so you have a problem-free boat dive. It typically includes the following four topics, among others:

Facility/boat orientation. This covers things like where the head and showers are, food concessions or coolers, where to stow things you want to stay dry or safe, where to find safety equipment and other information that makes your stay on the boat more enjoyable. You may also learn about areas that are off limits (such as an engine compartment) or restricted (such as staying out of the bunk area while wearing a wet exposure suit). If it's not obvious, the crew will recommend where to gear up.

General characteristics. If the information's available (it isn't always), the divemaster will brief you on the bottom type and topography to expect, the depth range, current speed and direction (if present), areas you may want to avoid and areas you may specifically want to be sure you see (where the good stuff is). The briefing usually covers interesting or helpful facts about the site, such as how it got its name or a summary of a wreck's history. It may cover sensitive natural and/or cultural features of the site (such as fragile corals or exposed shipwreck parts) as well as environmental regulations and other conservation practices applicable to the site. As necessary, the divemaster may suggest a dive plan and techniques and locations for entering and exiting the water. The divemaster may also suggest minimum experience/training for the dive, for options within the dive.

Buddy team considerations. Especially on *open* charters (anyone can sign on for a dive), the crew usually checks to be sure everyone has a buddy. If someone doesn't have a buddy, the divemaster may help unbuddied divers connect so they can find someone to dive with. With a closed boat (entire boat booked by a dive center or other group), buddy teams may be expected to be handled within the group.

It's typical to recommend that those inexperienced with the area try to dive with someone who is. The briefing may also review buddy team procedures, especially if there are any protocols unique to the area.

Communication, emergency procedures and general safety rules. Although much of this typically reviews what you already know as a certified diver, it's important to listen because it will also cover the specifics the crew uses with respect to them. During the briefing, the crew may review hand signals, especially if the divemaster will be leading a tour. It's typical to be reminded to always signal "okay" when you surface, and you may hear about recall procedures, the role of supervisory personnel, what to do in an emergency, out-of-air procedures and when to exit. An experienced divemaster won't reteach what you already know, but rather apply your basic diving knowledge to the specific circumstances of the dive.

After the briefing, you and your buddy plan your dive based upon the information in the briefing, as well as your own training, personal limits and experience you have with the local environment. Be sure to check your dive computer and the RDP no stop limits.

Suiting Up and Gearing Up

There's significant variation in how and when you suit up depending upon the boat size, the climate and the time from dock to dive. Similarly, how and when you get into your kit will depend upon the boat and the conditions.

Inflatables and small hard-hull day boats. With deck space at a premium in small vessels, it's typical to assemble and check your scuba kit before you leave the dock. Depending upon how much space you have, the weather, the surface conditions and how long before you reach the dive site, you may put on your exposure suit entirely, partly or not at all. In cool climates, you may dress into your dry suit for the entire ride (even a moderately long one) so you're comfortable even with wind and spray. In hot, tropical climates, if you have a long boat ride you may wait until you're on site so you don't overheat. A common in-between solution is to put on your wet suit, but leave it peeled down to your waist.

On site, with small boats there are two options for gearing up. One is to inflate the BCDs and put your scuba units over the side on a line. This frees the deck for getting into your exposure suit, etc. Then, enter the water and put your kit on at the surface. Alternatively, you can pull them back aboard, gear up and back roll in.

The other option (especially if you're already in your suit) is for buddy's to help each other into their kits and enter using the sitting back-roll. This is a particularly good strategy in rough conditions. Either way, be sure to conduct a predive safety check.

In cool climates that require dry suits, you may choose to wear your suit from the time you leave the dock until you return.

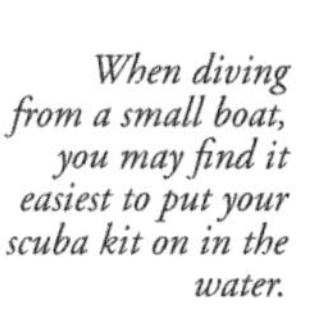

When diving from a small boat, you may find it easiest to put your scuba kit on in the water.

Cabin cruisers and live-aboards. Although you have more space on these larger boats, you still have to think about how you use that space. As discussed earlier, you'll normally set up your gear and leave it secured in the cylinder rack. On day trips you commonly do this before you leave the dock, and on overnight trips you typically set up for the day, but take everything apart, rinse and stow it overnight.

With the space available, you usually only get into your exposure suit before departure if the ride is going to be very short, or if you're diving in seas so rough that it will be difficult to do so offshore (this is for well seasoned divers, obviously). In warm climates and under sunny skies, you'll typically get into your exposure suit on deck, leaving your dry clothes forward or below decks. In cooler climates, you may dress into your dry suit undergarment in the salon or below decks, and put on the dry suit in a relatively sheltered area above deck.

In warm climates, you typically get into your exposure suit at the dive site on deck.

In cool climates, you may dress into your undergarment in the boat salon or below decks, and get into your dry suit in a relatively sheltered area above deck.

Gearing up depends partly on the vessel's configuration. On boats with seats in front of the cylinder racks, first put on your weight belt if you're wearing one. Then, release the cylinder bungee (if present), and slide into the BCD so you end up sitting with the cylinder in the rack. Buckle your BCD, and then secure your hoses and gauges. You'll be able to get completely ready to go, including most of your predive safety check, while remaining seated – especially advantageous when the boat's pitching on the waves. When it's time to dive, pull on your mask (you should have defogged it earlier, while prepping your scuba unit), but not your fins.

On boats with seats in front of the cylinder rack, you can usually get into all your gear except your fins while remaining seated.

Stand up carefully (if you forgot to release the bungee, this is when you find out and sheepishly ask someone to unhook it), helping and being helped by your buddy. Walk back to the entry area, complete your predive check (whatever you couldn't do while seated), and partially inflate your BCD. Put your fins on *last*, just before you enter the water, with your buddy helping steady you. Avoid walking on deck with fins on, because you can easily lose your balance and fall.

In some areas, large dive boats don't have seats in front of the cylinder racks. If this is the case, you and your buddy will lift and hold each other's scuba units so you kit up and perform your predive safety checks standing. You may be able to get into your scuba unit independently by balancing it on a sturdy rail (but don't do this in rough conditions because it may go over the side), but don't swing it over your head old school style. You may bonk someone in the head or lose your balance and fall because the boat rolled with your kit over your head.

On boats without seats in front of the cylinder racks, you and your buddy will help each other gear up while standing.

One note: Virtually all dive boats reasonably accommodate individual needs and will help you depart from the standard methods of gearing up, entering, exiting, etc. If you have a physical challenge or some other reason to do things differently, be sure to ask the crew and your buddy.

Non charter, Private Boats

The predive procedures when diving from private boats (which, in fact, most inflatables and hard-hull day boats are) are the same as from charter boats, but you have some additional considerations.

The first is that you never leave a vessel moored or anchored unattended. There should always be someone aboard who can operate the boat in case it breaks free, the anchor drags or the divers need help. This isn't always convenient, such as you have three divers in a small boat, but you can make it work: Diver A dives with Diver B while Diver C waits in the boat. For the second dive, A and C dive while B boat sits. Finally, A tends the boat while B and C dive together.

Never leave a boat unattended at anchor or while moored. There should always be someone who can operate it aboard.

It's also important to be flying an appropriate dive flag in accordance with the regulations for the area (as discussed earlier). Although as a diver you want to be sure to fly a dive flag for the safety benefits, it is the captain's *legal* responsibility.

Finally, when planning to dive from a private boat, consider enrolling in your local boating class and remember to pay special attention to the basic guidelines to boating safety outlined in this course.

Predive Roll Calls

You can expect the divemaster or crew to call roll before and after each dive from a charter dive boat. Particularly with a larger boat with many divers, this will be a formal gathering with the divemaster calling out names and listening for responses. If there are only a handful of passengers aboard, the divemaster may silently check off each name of every diver leaving and returning to the boat, but either way, this is an important standard safety procedure.

It is important to be present for roll call, before and after a dive. Never allow anyone to answer for you during a roll call. Be sure your name is called, and never answer for anyone else. Confusion about this has caused divers to accidentally get left at dive sites. It is your responsibility to take pre and post-dive roll calls seriously, and to be sure that you and only you answer when your name is called. This procedure is for your safety. (If it ever seems inconvenient – like you need to go to the head – just imagine how inconvenient it would be to surface in the middle of the ocean with the boat nowhere in sight.)

Exercise 8 - Charter Boat Boarding and Predive Procedures

1. The general boarding procedures for a charter dive boat include (check all that apply):
   - ☐ a. planning to arrive at least 30 minutes in advance.
   - ☐ b. stowing your gear according to crew instructions.
   - ☐ c. putting your personal gear where it will stay dry.
   - ☐ d. listening to predeparture briefings.

2. A dive boat area orientation usually covers (check all that apply):
   - ☐ a. a facility/boat orientation.
   - ☐ b. general characteristics of the dive site.
   - ☐ c. buddy team considerations.
   - ☐ d. communication, emergency procedures, and general safety rules.

3. Suiting up on a boat (check all that apply):
   - ☐ a. frequently takes place before you leave the dock when diving from a small boat.
   - ☐ b. may be affected by how long the boat ride is.
   - ☐ c. usually takes place at the dive site on large dive boats.
   - ☐ d. is never a good idea.

4. A predive roll call by divemasters or crewmembers is important
   - ☐ a. for your safety.
   - ☐ b. for saving time.
   - ☐ c. to lawmakers.
   - ☐ d. None of the above.

How'd you do?
1. *a, b, c, d.* **2.** *a, b, c, d.* **3.** *a, b, c.* **4.** *a.*

Boat Diving *Procedures*

Study Objectives

Underline/highlight the answers to these questions as you read:

1. What are the general guidelines for making entries from various types of boats?
2. What are *trip lines, gear lines, descent lines* and *current lines* used for?
3. What are the procedures for descending while boat diving?
4. In which direction should you generally head when boat diving?
5. What are the general guidelines for ascents while boat diving?
6. What are the general guidelines for exiting into a boat?

Boat Diving Entries

Here are the general procedures you follow when entering the water from most dive boats:

1. After your predive safety check, confirm with your buddy and the divemaster/boat crew that you're ready to enter the water.
2. Check that the entry area is clear of obstacles and other divers.
3. Partially inflate your BCD prior to entry.
4. Use your regulator during the entry. If you're putting on your scuba unit after you enter, breathe through your snorkel.
5. Hold your mask firmly as you enter (just like you practiced during the PADI Open Water Diver course).
6. After entering, signal that you're okay (assuming you are).
7. Have your buddy or the crew hand you accessories such as a camera, if any.
8. Move away from the boat/entry area so others can enter. Keep an eye on the boat because it may swing toward you.

Small boat entries. Chances are you already know the most commonly used boat entries. From small boats, you may perform a sitting back roll (i.e. rolling backward into the water) or a controlled seated entry (easing yourself in from a seated position) off the gunwale. Both entries are appropriate with your scuba on or off.

The sitting back roll is a popular entry from small boats.

Cabin cruiser and live-aboard entries. By far the most common entry from large charter boats is a giant stride. You may do this from the swim step, or from the side of the boat. The giant stride is a particular good choice for entries from a couple metres/a few feet above the water.

Sitting back roll entries and controlled seated entries aren't as common from large boats, but not unheard of. You may opt to back roll in rough conditions that make standing for the stride awkward, or because it's the most convenient entry for where you are on the boat. Controlled seated entries off the swim step are possible, and one choice for people with physical challenges.

Although the giant stride is the most popular entry from larger dive boats, a controlled seated entry off the boat's swim step may be an option if you prefer.

Boat Diving Lines

One thing that separates boat diving from shore diving is that boat diving usually involves descending, ascending and even moving horizontally through the use of various lines. In areas with excellent visibility and little or no current, the only line from the boat may be the mooring/anchor line, which you're already familiar with. Other areas, such as those with high current, diving may involve using multiple lines as part of your descent and ascents.

Gear lines. Gear lines are lines you use to tie off equipment in the water, usually off the side but sometimes off the transom. They're common in small boat diving (as previously described), but also used from all sized boats to suspend accessories like a camera for retrieval after you enter the water.

Tag lines. Tag lines may be used from any sized boat while anchored/moored in a current too strong to reasonably swim against at the surface. Tag lines run from the stern to the mooring/anchor line and allow you to pull yourself from the entry area to the mooring/anchor line. At the stern, the tag line may connect to the transom, or it may continue past the boat and connect to the current line. Ideally, a tag line attaches to the mooring/anchor line at about 5 metres/15 feet (accomplished by attaching the line and then letting out more mooring/anchor line). This starts your ascent as you pull yourself forward, plus makes extra room at the safety stop depth for several divers coming up. However, it's not always feasible to do this, in which case the tag line joins the mooring/anchor line at the surface.

Tag lines have differing names regionally. You may hear them called *swim lines* or (less politely) *granny lines*.

Current lines. Current lines float behind the boat, extending from the stern and terminating in a buoy. This line provides a larger/closer target for divers who accidentally ascend behind the boat (down current), or alongside the boat to one side. In the latter case, the divers swim across the current to reach the current line, which is much easier (and more likely to succeed) than trying to reach the boat.

You also use the current line as a place to wait for your buddy after you enter, and to wait your turn to exit after you come up. When the current is strong enough to require current lines (and tag lines), it's important to maintain line contact after entering, while descending, ascending and while waiting to exit. This is the only reliable way of being sure you don't get swept away from the boat and have to be picked up.

Current lines are also called *trail lines* or *stern lines*.

Trip lines. You don't see trip lines in most places, and they're less common than they once were thanks to the increase in moorings. Trip lines attach to the front of an anchor and rise to the surface supported by a buoy. The crew uses it to "trip" or release the anchor because they can pull the anchor backwards with it, unhooking it.

Divers sometimes use trip lines for descent or ascents, but only when there's little current. You don't want to pull on a trip line because you can dislodge the anchor, particularly a small one.

Descent lines. Descent lines are vertical weighted lines hanging from the boat, usually from the stern used for descent and ascent references. It usually doesn't reach all the way to the bottom because the weight will do a lot of damage as the boat swings back and forth on its mooring/anchor. Instead, it usually stops several metres/feet above the bottom.

Descent lines are commonly used when the boat moors/anchors in a way that allows it to sit directly over the dive site, with the mooring/anchor some distance away. They're also common in areas where you dive behind the boat, since the mooring/anchor line heads the wrong way.

Because they're not secured at the bottom, they're not very useful in anything but negligible current because they seldom have enough weight for this purpose.

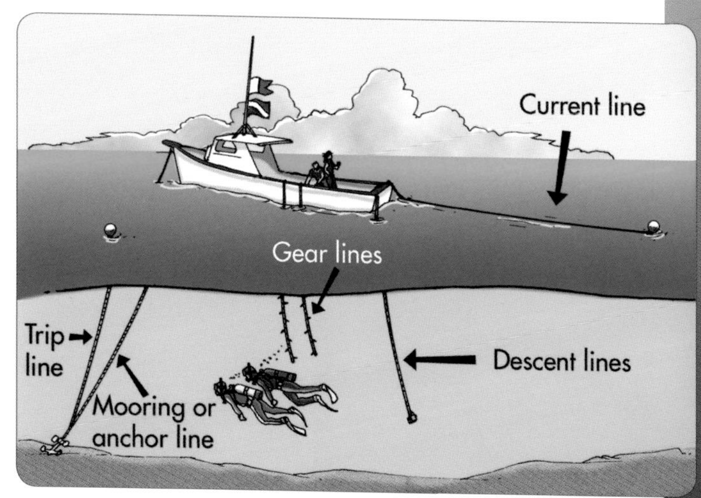

Common lines used in boat diving.

A strong current can push enough to lift the divers, line and weight almost to the surface. This is why the mooring/anchor line is a better place for safety stops in strong current.

Boat Diving Descents

The biggest difference between a shore diving descent and a boat diving descent is that when you're shore diving, you commonly start in shallow water and follow the bottom into deeper water. Boat diving, you're typically already in deeper water.

General procedures. Before descending, orient yourself to the boat's direction and/or the shoreline based on natural navigation or your compass. Note your air pressure, the time and where your buddy is.

When possible, descend along a line as a reference to provide comfort and orientation. This is especially beneficial if you can't see the bottom from the surface. If descending along an anchor line, use it only as a visual guide if there's little or no current because pulling on it could dislodge it. While this is unlikely with a very large anchor, it is possible with a small boat anchor. This isn't an issue with mooring lines, obviously, nor is a problem when the current is so strong that you must hang onto it as you descend. When there's current, there will be plenty of tension holding the anchor in place.

As you descend, maintain buddy contact. Watch your depth, time and air pressure. If you're descending by pulling yourself along a mooring line, watch where you put your hands so you don't accidentally get any marine life stings. Some mooring lines have extensive marine growth so, as discussed earlier; you may want to wear gloves.

When you descend along an anchor line with little or no current, use it as a visual reference, but avoid pulling on it so you don't accidentally dislodge it.

Mooring/anchor line descent. Most boat diving descents are along the mooring/anchor line, especially in areas with currents. In stronger currents that you can't reasonably swim against, the procedure is to enter the water next to the tag line (or by the current line in you have to wait for your buddy). Breathing from your regulator, you pull yourself to the mooring/anchor line, and then continue your descent hand-over-hand down it to the bottom, maintaining contact the entire time. If you don't keep a grip on it in strong current, you'll end up having to surface as quickly as you safely can and grab the current line. The current is usually much weaker at the bottom, allowing you to swim into it.

In stronger currents that you can't reasonably swim against, you enter the water next to the tag line and pull yourself to the mooring/anchor line. Maintain contact with the mooring/anchor line as you descend along it hand-over-hand to the bottom.

As you descend, be cautious because the anchor line will jerk up and down as the boat rises and falls on the swells. However, tension caused by current and chain at the base of the mooring/anchor line help reduce this. Unless there's almost no wind or current (which is rare), the mooring/anchor line isn't vertical, but angled due to scope, with a curve at the bottom caused by the weight of the chain. The straightening and bending of this curve helps dampen wave action.

When diving from an anchored boat, be alert for the boat needing to reanchor. It doesn't happen often, but if you suddenly feel the anchor line being hauled up, release it and swim clear.

Descent line descent. Make your way to the bottom along a stern-mounted descent line by following it as a visual or touch reference. Descent lines rise and fall with the boat, and they're far more affected by wave motion than mooring/anchor lines because they don't have the curve to dampen wave action. Since you don't use descent lines with much current, however, you don't typically need to hang onto one that's bouncing up and down.

Use a descent line as a visual or touch reference.

Free descent (no line). In many situations, you descend directly to the bottom without using a line at all. This is particularly true when you can see the bottom from the surface and there's little or no current. You can descend without a reference when you can't see the bottom, but watch your gauges and your buddies so you don't get disoriented in midwater. In any case, you and your buddy should keep track of each other, and be careful to watch your rate of descent.

On the Bottom

As you approach the bottom, control your buoyancy and avoid contact with anything fragile, such as reef organisms or shipwreck artifacts.

When you reach the bottom, you want to plan your dive so you end your dive at or near the boat. This avoids surface swims, which are more tiring and may present a hazard from boat traffic (use an inflatable signal tube if you must to be seen). When diving in strong current, ascending anywhere but along the mooring/anchor line risks ending up downstream and having to be picked up by the boat.

Most of the time, when you reach the bottom you swim into the current, which is generally ahead of the boat (the boat may sit at an angle to the current if there's a strong crosswind). By starting your dive into the current, it helps you rather than fights you on the way back.

Most of the time when boat diving, you swim into the current ahead of the boat.

In a few places, you dive behind the boat, between it and the shoreline. This is common, for example, where the bottom slopes steeply away from an island or reef and there's no current. One advantage of this is that you usually don't have to worry as much about boat traffic (though you should still be vigilant).

Because boat diving usually puts you right on or very close to the best diving, you don't need to go far and it's best not to. The farther you go, the harder it is to find your way back on the bottom. Turn the dive and head back with plenty of air and no stop time left. If you reach it with more air or time left than you expected, you can usually finish the dive in the immediate area around the boat before heading up.

Drift diving. Drift diving is a specialty beyond the scope of the PADI Boat Diver course. It involves diving in a strong current by riding with it rather than swimming against it, with the boat following you above. Many of the same boat diving procedures and principles you're learning in this course apply (so the PADI Boat Diver certification is an excellent one to have if you'll be drift diving), but drift diving uses specialized techniques for entering, exiting, staying in a group, streamlining to avoid accidental damage to the environment, and surfacing safely around a maneuvering boat. To learn more about drift diving, enroll in the Drift Adventure Dive and/or the PADI Drift Diver course.

Ascents

Boat diving ascents are usually the reverse of the descents. That is, if you descended along a line, you usually ascend along the same line. If you needed to maintain line contact on the way down due to current, you usually need to maintain line contact on the way up.

Start your ascent by noting your bottom time, air pressure and other information. As you ascend, remember S.A.F.E. concepts – Slowly Ascend From Every dive. This means no faster than 18 metres/60 feet per minute, or more commonly, an even slower rate as specified by your computer. Unless you're dealing with very low air or another problem, make a safety stop for at least three minutes at 5 metres/15 feet.

If possible, ascend using a visual reference such as the mooring/anchor line or descent line. When diving in stronger current, the procedure is to ascend the mooring/anchor line, hanging on to avoid being carried away in the current. Often, you simply climb the line, hand-over-hand, facing into the current with your feet behind you like a flag going up a mast. At 5 metres/15 feet (plus or minus if there are other divers in front of or behind you), simply stop climbing and hang on for your safety stop. After the stop, continue up, transfer to the tag line and follow it to the stern.

Whether you have a current or not, come up with your arm and hand extended upward, looking up and around. Rotate slowly for a clear view, and watch out for the boat bottom. Try to break the surface near the boat, which should have a dive flag up. This reduces risk from other boat traffic.

Avoid the propeller area at all times. Boat propellers easily maim and kill. Assume propellers will start turning at any time without warning.

If caught down current. If you get disoriented and can't locate the boat when diving in a current, ascend cautiously as far up current as you reasonably can. To reach the boat, don't fight the current, but swim *across it* to reach either the boat or the current line. If you miss, deploy your surface signaling device, establish buoyancy and signal the boat to pick you up. You may have to wait until they get everyone else aboard.

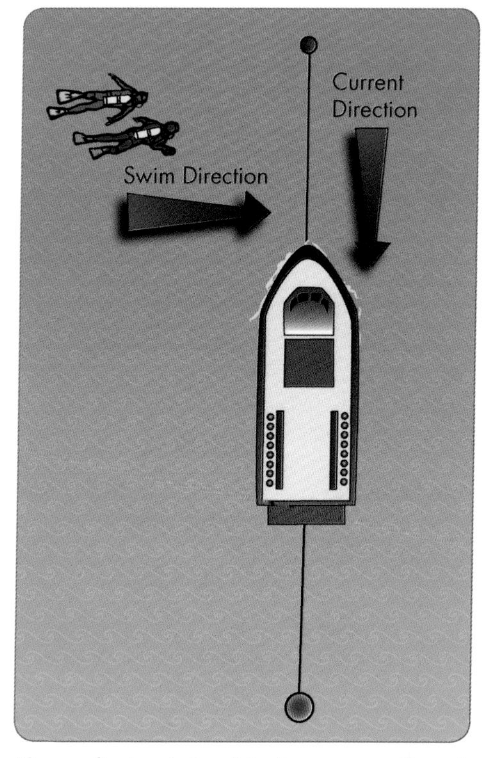

If you get disoriented when diving in a current, surface as far up current as you reasonably can, then swim across it to reach the current line.

Boat Diving Exits

Most dive boats have one, or at most two ladders, so you often have to wait your turn near the exit area (usually the stern). If there's a current, hang onto the current line. Establish buoyancy and, keep your mask on and your snorkel or regulator in your mouth while you wait. Stay well back from the exit area in case the diver ahead falls back in, or a cylinder drops out of a backpack.

If you have any accessories, you usually hand them up before starting your exit. Take your fins off only after making contact with the boat. When diving in currents, you may want to place your fins straps over your wrist (assuming they're strap fins) rather than pass them up. That way, you can pull them on and swim for the current line if you lose your grip or fall back in and start to get carried away from the boat. In any case, climb the boat ladder with your mask on and breathing from your regulator in case you fall back in. *Stay adapted to the water until you're completely clear of the water.*

Exit the water with your mask on, your regulator in your mouth and with your fins over your wrists. Stay adapted to the water until you're completely clear of the water.

Some boats – especially large ones that stand well above the water – have a swim step or stern platform you climb onto to exit. Time your exit with the swells, using the water to help lift you up and onto the platform.

With small boats like inflatables or other vessels without a ladder, you'll need to take your gear off in the water. You may also need to do this with some boats that have ladders that are too weak to support you with all your gear on – not unusual in tec diving.

In either situation, you'll get out of your weights and

When exiting onto a platform or swim step at or below water level, crawl onto the platform. Time lifting yourself up with the waves or swell, if present.

scuba in the water and either hand them up to someone on board, or tie them to a gear line to pull up after you get aboard. To get into a small boat, you kick (so keep your fins on) upward and push with your arms, turning so you end up seated on the side (inflatables) or transom (hard-hull day boat).

To get into a small boat without a ladder, kick up and push upward, turning so you end up seated on the side or stern.

Sun, Moon and Tides

On the oceans and even on some large lakes, the tides affect boating and diving. In some places, the tides rise and fall more than 10 metres/30 feet, and vessels can't enter or leave harbor at low tide without hitting the bottom. In other areas, tidal variation is minimal. Tides also influence anchoring; you have to leave enough scope for a rising tide, crossing shoals and leaving enough slack when docked to a pier that doesn't float and therefore rise and fall with the boat and tide.

As you may know, gravitational pull from the moon and sun cause the tides by pulling a bulge of water up in the seas. The bulge travels throughout the day as the earth rotates, causing daily tidal fluctuations. Depending upon the regional geography, some areas have a single high tide and low tide daily (called *diurnal* tide), others have two highs and lows (called *semidiurnal* tide), and yet others have two highs and lows of unequal strength (called *mixed* tide).

The relative height of the high tide and the degree of difference between high and low vary seasonally depending upon the relative positions of the sun and moon. The moon has the most effect on the tides because it is much closer to earth, but the sun can strengthen or somewhat neutralize its effect, depending upon their positions.

Spring tides have the highest tides and the greatest variations. At these times, the sun and moon align so they pull together and maximize the tidal bulge. Neap tides occur when the sun and moon sit at roughly a 90-degree angle. In this case, the sun's pull cancels out the moons to some degree, reducing the tidal variation and the height of high tide. Throughout the 28-day lunar cycle, the tides continuously transition from spring to neap tide and back.

To learn more about tides, see the Aquatic Realm section of the *Encyclopedia of Recreational Diving.*

Exercise 9 - Boat Diving Procedures

1. General guidelines for entering the water from a boat include (check all that apply):
   - ☐ a. breathing from your regulator.
   - ☐ b. signaling that you're okay after entering.
   - ☐ c. moving away from the entry area so others can enter.
   - ☐ d. having someone hand you accessories after entering.

2. A _______ line is used to retrieve the anchor, and a ___________ line helps you reach the mooring/anchor line in a strong current:
   - ☐ a. trip, current
   - ☐ b. trip, tag
   - ☐ c. current, trip
   - ☐ d. tag, current

3. When descending on a boat dive (check all that apply):
   - ☐ a. avoid using a reference of any kind.
   - ☐ b. maintain buddy contact.
   - ☐ c. maintain line contact in strong current.
   - ☐ d. be cautious regarding rising and falling mooring/anchor lines or descent lines.

4. When boat diving, when you reach the bottom you generally head
   - ☐ a. down current.
   - ☐ b. across the current.
   - ☐ c. into the current.
   - ☐ d. None of the above.

5. When ascending on a boat dive (check all that apply):
   - ☐ a. plan your dive so you ascend near the boat.
   - ☐ b. maintain buddy contact.
   - ☐ c. maintain line contact in strong current.
   - ☐ d. ascend no faster the 18 metres/60 feet per minute, or slower if required by your computer.

6. The guidelines for exiting the water onto a dive boat include (check all that apply):
   - ☐ a. keeping your mask on and breathing from your regulator or snorkel.
   - ☐ b. staying out from under divers climbing a boat ladder.
   - ☐ c. removing your scuba kit in the water when diving from a small boat.
   - ☐ d. handing up accessories before exiting.

How'd you do?
1. *a, b, c, d.* **2.** *b.* **3.** *b, c, d.* **4.** *c.* **5.** *a, b, c, d.* **6.** *a, b, c, d.*

Post-Dive Procedures

Study Objectives

Underline/highlight the answers to these questions as you read:

1. How should you repack and stow your gear after a dive from various sized boats?
2. Why should you listen to post-dive roll calls by divemasters or crew members?

Packing and Stowing Your Equipment

Once you're back on the boat, watch your balance, minimize how far you walk and get seated and/or out of your gear as soon as possible, especially if the boat's rolling a lot. Watch out for slipping on a wet deck, and secure your cylinder as soon as you're out of your kit. Don't drop your cylinder or weights on the deck – doing so can damage the deck, plus it's a good way to injure someone.

Remember that space is a premium, just like before the dive. On most charter boats, you'll put your kit where you started. If you'll be making another dive, put your gear on or near your gear bag, or put your gear directly into your bag if you're done diving for the day. Some boats have tags or procedures that alert the crew to refill your cylinder.

When diving from a small boat and exiting by taking your gear off in the water, you'll usually stow your other equipment, then pull your scuba equipment aboard. You may leave your scuba assembled until you return to the dock, and depending upon your exposure suit and the climate, you may keep your exposure suit on, too.

After the dive, get out of your gear as soon as possible, and be sure to secure your cylinder so it can't fall or roll.

Post-Dive Roll Call

As you learned earlier, after the dive the divemaster or crew will check to be sure everyone's aboard.

With smaller boats and only a handful of divers, the divemaster may do this quietly, but on larger boats the procedure usually involves a formal roll call. Again, be visually present for the roll call. **Do not answer for someone else, and do not have anyone answer for you**. Should you not be aboard, you don't want to be left behind because someone answered for you.

The divemaster may also give a debriefing. If so, listen because the debriefing may also be the briefing for the next dive (especially if the boat's not going to move), and it may include arrival/docking instructions. It's often easier to brief you on these at the dive site because it's quieter without the engines running.

Exercise 10 - Post-Dive Procedures

1. When repacking and stowing your gear after a boat dive, you should (check all that apply):
   - ☐ a. remember that space is still at a premium.
   - ☐ b. stow your gear directly into your bag if you're done diving for the day.
2. If you can't be on deck during a post-dive roll call, you should have someone answer for you.
   - ☐ True ☐ False

How'd you do?

1\. *a.* **2.** *False. Never have someone answer for you at roll call. Be on deck for the roll call because its purpose is your safety.*

Boat Diver Specialty Course

Open Water Dives

The following outlines the two dives you'll make as part of your PADI Boat Diver Specialty course. Your instructor may rearrange skill sequences in each dive, or may add more dives as necessary to meet your needs, desires, course requirements and environmental conditions.

Dive 1

- Knowledge Review/Briefing
- Predive Procedures – Above Water Skill Practice
- Dive 1 Tasks
  - Identify the following areas of the specific boat used on the dive: bow, stern, starboard, port, entry area, exit area and area to stow diving equipment.
  - Locate important emergency/safety equipment aboard the boat (such as: first aid kit, oxygen, AED, dive flag, radio, life jackets or other flotation devices, and fire extinguisher).
  - Perform a proper entry, specific to the type of boat used on the dive.
  - Perform a safety stop at 5 metres/15 feet for at least three minutes.
  - Perform a proper exit, specific to the type of boat used on the dive.
- Post-dive Procedures
- Debrief
- Log Dive

Dive 2

- Knowledge Review/Briefing
- Predive Procedures – Above Water Skill Practice
- Dive 2 Tasks
  - Demonstrate the ability to construct a dive plan that takes into account the type of boat used and the diving environment.
  - Demonstrate the ability to apply the knowledge learned from the course to dive from the type of boat used.
- Post-dive Procedures
- Debrief
- Log Dive

Name ____ Date ____________

Knowledge Review — Part I

Note to the student: The first half of this Knowledge Review is the same Knowledge Review in the Boat Diving section of *Adventures in Diving*. If your instructor has the first half on file from your PADI Adventure Diver or PADI Advanced Open Water Diver course, your instructor may have you complete only the second half of this Knowledge Review.

Answer the following questions and bring this completed Knowledge Review with you to your next training session.

1. On the illustration, label the following: bow, stern, port, starboard, windward and leeward.

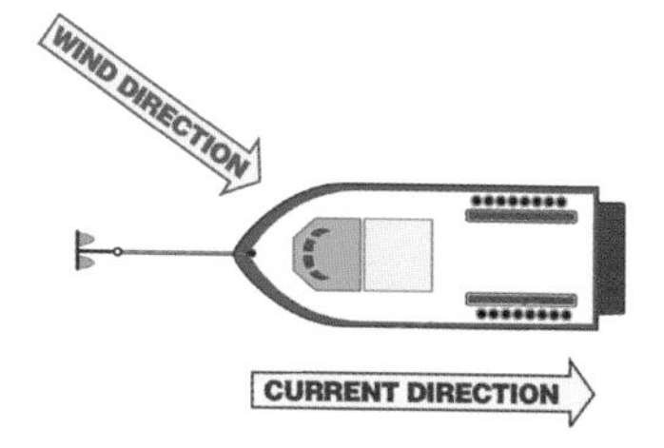

2. List eight pieces of emergency equipment commonly found on dive boats.

   1. ____________________ 2. ____________________
   3. ____________________ 4. ____________________
   5. ____________________ 6. ____________________
   7. ____________________ 8. ____________________

3. Describe how to help prevent seasickness, and what to do if you become seasick.

4. Describe the general boarding procedure for a typical charter boat.

5. On most dive boats be sure to work from your dive bag and not take up ___________.

6. Explain the general guidelines for making proper entries from various types of boats.

7. Explain the location and purpose for trip line, gear line, tag line, and current line.

   Trip line:

   Gear line:

   Tag line:

   Current line:

8. Describe the procedures for making a free descent from a boat.

9. What are the general guidelines for making a proper exit into a charter boat?

10. Explain why you should listen to post-dive roll calls by divemasters or crewmembers.

Student Diver Statement:

Any questions I answered incorrectly or incompletely, I've had explained to me, and I understand what I missed.

Name ____ Date ______________

Name ______________________________ Date ______________

Knowledge Review — Part II

Answer the following questions and bring this completed Knowledge Review with you to your next training session.

11. List five advantages of diving from a boat.

    1. ______________________________
    2. ______________________________
    3. ______________________________
    4. ______________________________
    5. ______________________________

12. List three features you would expect from virtually any dive boat.

    1. ______________________________
    2. ______________________________
    3. ______________________________

13. Provide a brief description (types of crafts, use, and size) of the four general categories of dive boats.

    Inflatables:

    Hard-hull day boats:

    Cabin cruisers:

    Live-aboards:

14. Explain why there are navigational rules of the road.

15. What are navigational charts and why are they important?

16. Who is responsible for, and what is your responsibility during docking and undocking the boat?

17. Describe how to use a marine radio in case of an emergency, and explain what information you should be prepared to give.

18. List four considerations when selecting a mooring or an anchorage for diving.

    1. ____
    2. ____
    3. ____
    4. ____

19. How do you prepare your equipment and yourself for a boat dive?

20. List the four topics typical of a boat dive orientation.

    1. ____
    2. ____
    3. ____
    4. ____

Student Diver Statement:

Any questions I answered incorrectly or incompletely, I've had explained to me, and I understand what I missed.

Name ____ Date ________________